George + Patty McLarty

HOW MY WORLD TURNS

Eileen Fulton

as told to BRETT BOLTON

HOW MY
WORLD TURNS

TAPLINGER PUBLISHING COMPANY
NEW YORK

ISBN 0-8008-3970-6
LIBRARY OF CONGRESS CATALOG CARD NUMBER 73-125302
PUBLISHED SIMULTANEOUSLY IN THE DOMINION OF CANADA
BY BURNS & MAC EACHERN LTD., ONTARIO
DESIGNED BY CHARLES KAPLAN
PRINTED IN THE UNITED STATES OF AMERICA

TO

My Mother and Daddy for making me possible
Erna Phillips for making "Lisa" possible
Brett Bolton for making this book possible
Dori Davis for making all impossibles possible

HOW MY WORLD TURNS

1

When the part of Lisa in *As the World Turns* was offered to me, I was told she was to be a temporary character, a mere foil for the young Bob Hughes, who had just entered college. The Lisa the writers had created was made of "sugar and spice and everything nice." I wanted the part. It would be a good break for me, but inwardly I was repelled by this character. She *was* me and I was sick of her. Sweetness and goodness had been shoved down my throat all my life and, at that time, I was rebelling against everything I had been taught. I was fighting for my identity. The producers, of course, had no way of knowing that my own world was spinning, colliding against tradition, my family, myself. So, at every opportunity to make her just the least bit conniving, I played it to the hilt. The writers saw that what I was doing worked. The girl who was to be written out in a few short weeks suddenly started getting more material and I began to create the lovable monster she has since become.

At that same time, I was making a Warner Brothers' movie, *Girl of the Night*. I played the leading "lady" who was a tramp. A hooker. Her name, interestingly enough, was Lisa, too. How

I loved making that film. It was the first time in my life, as a person or as an actress, I had ever been given a chance to be bad. You see, I am a minister's daughter. And I was never allowed to forget it. I always had to be perfect. No easy task, especially when you're little. My childhood was a trying time for me because I was looked upon by other children as being different. By the time I got into my teens I really was an outcast. I was *the* minister's daughter. Do you know what it's like to walk down the street and see all the kids hide because here you come, Miss Priss Margaret? "She's as pure as the driven snow, you know." I wasn't. I was a walking atom bomb. Behind that smile-chiseled mask was a teary-eyed girl who longed to be like everybody else. I wanted to go to the drugstore and sip Cokes and flirt with the boys like all the girls did but I could not. I wanted to smoke, smooch and swear, but I could not. I always had to think of what it might do to Daddy's career. So, out of an ever-growing loneliness, I retreated more and more into a world of fantasy. Would you believe I was still playing dress up when I was in the eighth grade? The only thing that kept that ticking bomb from going off was my passionate desire to someday be an actress. In portraying someone other than myself I was relieved of my obligation. I was at liberty to let go. I could be saint or sinner without being fearful of tainting my father's good name.

A minister's life is never his own. It is a gypsy life. By the time I was seventeen, we had moved nine times. Every September my daddy attended the Western North Carolina Methodist Conference, and it was at this time the district superintendent determined who was to be moved to another church, who was to remain because the congregation wanted it that way and who was to be removed to another church because the congregation did not like his brand of medicine. But even if all was well, all around, a Methodist minister never remained in one church for more than four years.

The bishop and his cabinet make all final decisions as to what preacher goes where, who should move and so forth. They try to put the minister in the kind of congregation he suits best. Some ministers are hellfire and brimstone. You know, "Brothers and sisters, I am here to save your souls—" If the church likes that kind of soul-saving, then the bishop sees to it the right man for the job is sent. Occasionally, mistakes are made and a quiet-speaking shepherd finds himself in high grass and has to lean on his staff a lot until they can get him out of there.

My Daddy likes a formal kind of service where he wears the pulpit gown, and the choir is in robes. I call it High Methodist. This type of service is very much like the Episcopalian.

It seemed a natural choice for my father to choose the ministry because his father, the late Emmett McLarty, was a minister and Daddy's brother Emmett was also.

Grandfather McLarty was famous all over the South and had some of the finest churches in his day. He was quite spectacular and, brother, when he got through with you, your bones rattled trying to contain that throbbing soul of yours. He was all thunder and lightning and could be heard above the sound of an organ, over and beyond the church and into the meanest corners of the town. He was more of a Shakespearean type preacher. Daddy has a gentle delivery. He is more of the method actor type. I preferred Daddy's approach, but I've since learned to use a little of Grandfather's thunder and lightning, too.

When I was born, Mother and Daddy had been married six years so I was a most welcomed child. My arrival took place in Mission Hospital in Asheville. I was the "star" of the Glenns (Mother's people) and the McLartys because I was the first grandchild. I was the center of attention and loved it. But being the center of so much attention took its toll when I grew older and sought out children of my own age.

Mother called me Sweetie, as did all my relatives, and Daddy, to balance me out, called me Old Girl. The neighbors called me Little Margaret because Mother, Nanny (my maternal grandmother) and I all had the same name: Margaret Elizabeth.

Mother is a schoolteacher and Nanny was, too, so everyone assumed I would follow in their footsteps. I almost did. Between Mother and Daddy I got plenty of discipline. I learned to control my body, mind, and soul. The one thing I could never keep a tight rein on was my fantastic imagination.

As an infant, I was very happy and I remember a great deal about my babyhood. People say babies are not aware of what's

going on, that they don't notice things and certainly don't remember their first year of existence. Well, that's not true. I
remember many things. When I mentioned this recently to my
mother she said, "Oh, now Sweetie, you just imagine that you
remember." Then I told her of a time when I was about eight
or nine months old and had diarrhea and she took me to see a
Dr. Elias. He had a doll that he kept on a high shelf wrapped
in brown paper and while he was examining me he would let me
play with the doll. "How could you remember that? You were
too little." I went on to tell her that I had been kept on a diet
of rice—no milk. And how delighted I was not to have to drink
milk because I hated it. Loved rice and still do. If I concentrated,
I don't doubt I could recall the coziness of Mother's womb.

I also recall my emotional reactions to the sound of words and
my exasperation in trying to make myself understood when first
beginning to learn to talk. I loved the sound of Old Girl. It had
a nice, round, smooth feeling to it which I loved hearing and
later associated with marbles and things that felt smooth to the
touch. Sweetie always made my jaws hurt and still does. Perhaps
that's why today I seldom use the word sweet. Or maybe it's just
because I never wanted to be.

I certainly remember being capable of reasoning and following
through with a plot when I was about a year old. I was learning
to talk but could not for the life of me say the word water.
I called water ogga. Now, I don't know if such a word ever
existed in some long forgotten language or not, nor am I sure that
I don't believe in reincarnation because many of the things I did
and many of the images I entertained myself with might well
have been past life experiences, but be that as it may, the word
ogga was understood by my parents to mean water.

One afternoon I had been tucked into my crib for the usual
nap time and in their absence I grew thirsty. I began to jump up
and down in the crib yelling for my ogga. No one would pay
me any attention as they probably thought it another excuse to
get out of sleepy-bye. I continued to project louder and louder,
jumped higher and higher as my anger mounted along with my
thirst. Suddenly the bedsprings broke, the bed collapsed. My
parents bolted into the room and there I sat, red-faced and fright-

ened on my bed, which was now on the floor. Poor Sweetie/Old Girl was bounced and hugged and finally given water. I was also given a lovely car ride while Daddy repaired the bed. Nap time was never to be skipped so Mother put me on the back seat, covered me up and drove slowly around the neighborhood while the lulling motion of the car drew me into a delightful dreamy sleep. The plot had begun. I reasoned that any time I wanted to go for a car ride I would simply break the bed and it worked for a time until they caught on.

My recollection of the discomfort of diapers is quite clear. I hated diapers. It made walking all the more difficult. I hated clothes. They were confining. Infants have a great respect for simplicity. They need few creature comforts and clothing is one thing they can nicely do without. A baby is in harmony with nature and has need of no further essentials to its well-being than being free of cumbersome attire. I, like all babies, loved being naked.

During my diaper days I, for a considerable time, had been clever enough to keep my nudity from Mother. Each day, when the weather permitted, she would park me in our lovely backyard, which was fenced in to prevent me from wandering while she tended to house chores. When I thought she was busy elsewhere and out of sight, I would carefully wriggle the diaper down, sail the dress over my head and freedom was mine. I made certain I stayed out of her line of vision and would spend the time allowed me happily entertaining myself in the way of all children, and when Mother would call me to "Come on in now," I would tug up the diaper, get back into the dress and go in, for the most part, the way I went out.

One afternoon, unbeknownst to me, a group of nice ladies from Daddy's church paid Mother a call. They said, "Mrs. McLarty, we realize you have your own ideas about bringing up children, but do you think it wise to let Little Margaret run around out there without a stitch on?" They marched my amazed Mother out the kitchen door and there in the farthest corner of the backyard beneath a big oak tree was me—Sweetie/Old Girl/Little Margaret—bending over, her pretty curls swaying, her bare bottom up, as she closely inspected a flower. Gasps were heard all around and I spied Mother from between my legs. I was caught. I froze. I knew that when I stood up that bare bottom of mine was going to burn.

Mother thanked the nice ladies and, wagging a finger at me, followed the committee back into the house, got out a basket of pins while the onlookers looked, nodding and tisking, and charged out in the yard after me. I grabbed my bottom and shook a lot. She did not spank me, which I was very thankful for. She put that diaper back on and pinned it in a dozen places, shoved the dress down over my head and that finger started wagging again. "Going without clothes is a no-no. Now, don't you ever do that again!" I gave her my dearest smile and tilted my head demurely. The ladies were satisfied and left.

I idled about, close to the house for some time, standing on tiptoe to determine Mother's whereabouts. When I thought guard duty was over I sailed the dress over my head and unpinned the diaper in a dozen places. In my frenzy, and not being very handy with pins at that time, I drew blood. Well, Mother is no fool. Now that she had been alerted to the fact that her Sweetie was a stripper, she came back to the kitchen to have a look-see. This time adhesive tape was applied. Again, when she was out of sight, I ripped off the tape, taking my flesh with it. I learned that day there is always a price to pay for freedom.

After a few days of trying to outdo Mother, I won. She gave up and so did the nice ladies. But winter was coming and Mother was worried because in Asheville the temperature drops below zero and she was afraid her Sweetie would get pneumonia.

I was highly allergic to pajamas and as winter approached Mother and Daddy held nightly conferences on how they would keep me from freezing to death in the long cold months that lay ahead. Suddenly they pounced on the solution: The dear old pajamas with trap door and feet. Add to the zipper a lightweight, tiny lock and Sweetie/Old Girl would remain bound for a good night's sleep. Only a Houdini could get out of those pajamas.

My room was actually the sun parlor and it did get a bit chilly in there, but I was a very healthy child (due to the fact that my body was conditioned) so the first cold day, Mother encased me in the mummy suit, locked the zipper, put me to bed for my afternoon nap, opened a few windows because she believed in fresh air, kissed me, bid me pleasant dreams and, humming happily, left me to my nap without further fear of her Sweetie catching pneumonia. But then she heard me squealing and giggling, which told her I was out of my clothes and, sure enough, there I stood, my pajamas hanging around my neck. I had escaped through the trap door. Mother gave up on me, kept the windows closed and prayed often.

By the time I reached the age of two, I had become civilized enough to know that church was not the place for running around naked. My parents knew they could trust me in church so one Sunday, when I was two, I gave my first public performance. All pink and pretty in frills and bows I stood on Daddy's pulpit and sang a song: "Shortnin' Bread." The congregation thought Little Margaret was just adorable and, when I finished my song, I bowed and they clapped. I screamed. I had never heard anyone clap in a church before. It sounded like a spanking. Daddy held me, Mother held me. I sputtered between sobs, "They're spanking me—" Daddy laughed, the congregation laughed and Mother bounced me, explaining as she carried me off that they liked my singing. Already the actress, I dried my tears quickly and waved to my audience as Mother took me home.

Uncle Tokie, Mother's brother, gave me a dog that year. She was a beautiful cocker spaniel and I named her Mickey. That was the happiest moment of my new life. There is nothing more fulfilling for a child than having an animal for a friend.

The day Uncle Tokie brought her to me, I took her in the kitchen to feed her. She didn't know enough to stop eating and I didn't know enough to stop feeding her. After all the food, I gave her something to wash it down. First, chocolate milk, then buttermilk, and then just milk. She suddenly started howling and trying to walk toward the door, but her stomach was dragging on the floor. She was dying, but I didn't know I had fed her to death! Uncle Tokie came running in and lifted her in the air, turned her upside down, and smacked her on the backside to get her to throw up. She did, and managed to survive what was about to be her "last supper." I decided that mothers knew best about feeding dogs as well as children, so I left Mickey's menu to Mother after that.

I loved her and she loved me. We were inseparable. We understood each other. For one thing, we both wanted to get out of the yard and go somewhere and meet people. We tried digging under the fence but got nowhere. Then I discovered my feet fit in the holes in the wire fence. Freedom at last. I climbed up the fence a number of times, instructing Mickey to do likewise. She finally caught on and Mother happened to look out the window to see me stark naked, that famous backside of mine glistening like marble under the glare of the morning sun, and Mickey climbing right behind me.

Daddy built a new fence.

Mickey intrigued me for a lot of reasons. One was that she could do her business in the yard. I was always so proud of her because I was made to feel I had done something wonderful when I made my push-hards, as I called it. One day, feeling very proud of her job, I thought I would make one, too. I did and, wanting an audience, called the neighbors on each side of our house to come see my push-hards. They came asking, "What are push-hards?" I gleefully pointed to Mickey's. "There's Mickey's and there's mine. Mine's bigger!" They hotfooted it into my house calling to Mother about "your daughter the disgrace." I soon learned dogs have certain privileges that people do not have.

Children are the true scientists. Their young minds are illumined with wonder. Every discovery demands an answer. When I was three I was very interested in bodies and one day my friend Marvin, who was also three, came to visit me. Mickey, Marvin and I were out in the yard playing when all of a sudden he said, "I have to make." He did. I was very puzzled. I said, "I can't do that." He said, "You can so. All you have to do is take it out and shoot it over there." I was fascinated by it and he was just as fascinated because he didn't know I didn't have what he had and I showed him. Then I went racing in the house and asked Mother, "How in the world did this happen that Marvin can make a nice little stream out there and I can't?" I stamped my feet in fury. "Marvin's got something I haven't!" Mother laughed, "Honey, you've got something Marvin doesn't have so don't let it worry you. But from now on, like all ladies do, you come in the house as you know to do when you have to go and if Marvin feels like he has to go, you let me know and I'll take him in the house, too." After that, I knew there was a difference between boys and girls and I wanted to know why.

Mother has always been marvelous about explaining things to me and I thought she gave my question a very good answer. "Because of the difference, babies are born. When boys and girls grow up, they get married and the girl gets a seed and the boy fertilizes it for her and that's how babies are born."

By this time Mother had discovered the trick to keeping me in clothes was to let me wear hers. Playing dress up became my favorite pastime and I continued to play it into my adult life. I, indeed, was one child born to be an actress.

One day I put on a beautiful nightgown of Mother's and went next door to visit Mrs. Fedder. I knocked and she opened the door with, "Oh, my goodness, go home and get dressed!" I said, "But I am dressed, Mrs. Fedder. I've come for tea." And she gasped, "You go home and get dressed. It's indecent to go around like that. You can't have tea with me until you put on some clothes." My temper was rising. "This is my evening dress as anyone can see, Mrs. Fedder!" She huffed and we had a good fight. I was so upset and Mother called me home. "Sweetie, she doesn't know how to play your game." That's when I began to understand that most grownups do not understand children.

I shall never forget the day Mother found it difficult to understand me. So that Mother could afford to have her hair done once a month (she had long, beautiful brown hair) she had to save her money. She had to save to buy cold cream, too. She took great pride in her skin and her hair, as well she should. My mother is still a lovely lady. Well, one day I sneaked into her room while she was out of sight and started inspecting her dresser. First, I opened a little box of pale lavender powder and tasted it. Bitter. I threw it on the floor and it spilled out. Next, I opened a jar of cold cream and tasted that. Delicious. The texture remotely reminded me of ice cream. So, I proceeded to eat the cold cream. As I was running my finger around the jar, getting the last of it, Mother walked in. She saw her precious powder spilled and the hard-to-come-by cream jar empty. She stood there and wept like a little girl. That was the first time I ever hurt her. I felt awful. More than my emotions were involved. I thought I was going to be sick. So I cried, too. But from cold cream I went to Ivory soap.

One day, just after this little feast of mine, while Mother was giving me a bath, the phone rang and she went to answer it. When she came back she saw the soap floating with all four corners bitten off. I started to say something because I knew she *knew*, but when I opened my mouth to defend myself, soap bubbles came out. My throat was killing me, but I couldn't cry because every time I opened my mouth—bubbles. It was only a matter of minutes before a lot more than bubbles came out. Mother was afraid I was going to die and I was afraid I would not get over the soap scene in time for our appointment. I was to have my picture taken, which I loved because it was like being a movie star. I willed myself well in time to pose for the photographer. (Interesting that my show, As the World Turns, is sponsored by Procter & Gamble, makers of Ivory, which I, to this day, cannot bear to use because my recall is so vivid. Eating soap can make you very sick.)

Then there was the time when I didn't understand Mother. Each night after I had been put to bed, Mother would sit beside me, tell me a story and then sing me to sleep with "Silent Night." One such evening, I said, "Why does anybody have to sleep in a bowl of peas?" Mother's pretty face took on a show of surprise, "What do you mean?" I said, "Sleep in heavenly peas?" That little bit of dialogue became a parlor panic.

That same year we got something we had long wished for: a refrigerator. In a Methodist parsonage one does not always have the finer things in life, but finally we got a refrigerator. Daddy carried it in on his back. I thought he was the strongest man in the world, as did all the neighbors because Preacher McLarty was called upon frequently to repair more than their souls. He was the local electrician and carpenter. A handy-man minister. You can't hardly find that kind anymore. Preacher James McLarty, my daddy, was the David who killed Goliath, my knight in shining armor. He was the most handsome man in the whole world to me. From my height, he appeared a giant, but in fact, he is not tall. He's five feet nine inches, and Mother, being tall, always wears low heels because he does not like her to appear taller than he. But, the day we got the refrigerator, the icebox was put out on the back porch. The next afternoon, that icebox almost became my coffin. I was playing hide-and-seek with some of the older children in the neighborhood and they decided a good place to hide me would be in the icebox so they put me in and shut the door. I waited a few minutes, giggling, but then time started to go by and nobody came for me. I grew frightened; it was dark in there, and I banged on the door, yelling, but nobody came. Soon breathing became difficult and then I didn't care anymore. I fell asleep. Suddenly the door opened and one of the big girls dragged me out. "Don't you ever dare tell your mother we put you in there!" Obviously, I had been forgotten for a while. I never played that game again and today I will not use a closet until an electric light has been installed.

A few weeks after my near death, Mother became ill and had to go to the hospital for an operation. Nanny, my grandmother, whom I worshipped and adored, took me every day to see her. Playing dress up, as I said, was always my favorite game and Nanny, understanding how important it was to me, would change the flowers on my little white hat each day so I felt like I was wearing a new outfit when I went to visit Mother.

When Mother came home, Susie came, too. Susie was to be our maid until Mother regained her strength. Daddy could not afford a maid but, until Mother got well, he had no choice. Susie was black, beautiful, young and fun. She wore crisp uniforms and I loved the way they smelled.

Christmas was on its way and Mother asked me what I wanted. I loved Susie so I wanted a colored baby doll more than anything else in the world. Having the doll would be like loving and caring for Susie. So, when Mother sent Susie out to do her Christmas shopping she told her to please find Sweetie a colored baby doll.

The most exciting holiday of the year arrived and I got my doll. Naturally, I named her Susie.

I have always been jealous of the people I love and Susie made the grave mistake one day of bringing her little boy to the house. She had no one to leave him with that morning and it was perfectly logical that the child could be entrusted to Sweetie's tender care for the day. Susie had never mentioned to me that she had a child. Had I known, I would have been prepared to cope with my emotions but I was unaware of his existence so shock set in when they arrived. There he stood, beside her. My rival. My Susie had a baby and no doubt loved him far more than she loved me. I battled against my jealousy and really tried to love him. He was adorable and I loved his skin, but he wanted all my toys and took everything away from me without asking. I wanted to give them to him, but he didn't wait for an offer and that made me mad. I stopped fighting my emotions and fought him. We had a terrible brawl, Mickey hid and Susie came running out and broke it up. I babbled, "You love him more'n you love me!" Susie went back in and said to Mother, "What in the world is wrong with Sweetie? She has never acted like this with other children." Mother laughed, all wise. "I'm afraid she's jealous of your boy." True. Sharing my love was very difficult for me in those days yet I desperately wanted a baby brother or sister.

September came and Susie left. For a time I thought my heart would break. Susie had to look for other employment because we were soon to move to Winston-Salem.

Shortly after my fourth birthday I decided to put on a show for Mother while she was busy in the kitchen. I had seen many shows at church so I made footlights out of empty milk bottles and lined them up in front of the kitchen door. I bowed first as I knew to do and waited for Mother to applaud, then I started singing and whirling, got dizzy and fell over the milk bottles. The bottles broke and I cut an artery in my knee. The blood flowed and Mother almost fainted. She could not stop the bleeding and she could not drive me to the hospital because she had to keep applying fresh compresses to my knee. She called Daddy and he came running. That was the only way he could get there because he walked the mile to church every day to save gas. Times were tough but I was never made to feel it. So, he ran all the way home and drove me to the hospital. I remember all of it. Getting a lot of stitches, waking up. What I didn't know is that I almost died.

I was very proud of my scar because it looked like a half moon and I would show it to everybody without being asked. "I've got a scar just like the moon in the sky." I guess in my young mind I figured since I wanted to be a movie star, you can't be a star unless there's a moon around. (I still have the habit of touching that scar before doing an audition or a new part in a play.)

The month of September was a very traumatic time for me because I knew Daddy had been given a new church in Winston-Salem. He didn't want to go and certainly we didn't want to leave, but it was a promotion for him and, besides, a minister has no choice in the matter.

One afternoon I was sitting in the house feeling sorry for myself because what would I do without Nanny and Marvin and the people I knew so well when I heard on the radio, "Now children, get pencil and paper. We are going to teach you how to make a castle." I loved to play make-believe and was always pretending to be a queen in a castle so I flew to get a pencil and paper and raced back to the radio. "Now, you take one old box and . . ." I was mortified. I had forgotten I didn't know how to write! I realized for the first time in my life I had attempted something I was not equipped to do. That experience made a permanent impression on me, because from that day on I never approached anything without being prepared for it.

When we moved to Winston-Salem, Mother was still recuperating from the operation and was too weak to chase after me and take care of us, so Daddy brought Reesie to run things for a while. Reesie wasn't as much fun as Susie because she didn't know how to play my games but she did teach me to bake cakes. This made me feel very grown-up and I was now beginning to identify strongly with my mother. I was becoming a lady. I had to. But the fact that my daddy was a minister, in the full connotation of the word, I did not grasp until I started school.

A few weeks after we arrived, there was a big revival meeting at Daddy's new church, which was next door to our parsonage. My very famous grandfather was to give one of his thunder and lightning sermons and people came from all over North Carolina to hear him. That was the night I decided I was now grown-up so I prepared myself for my "coming-out party."

Earlier that same afternoon, Mother had let me take a look at her prized evening gown which she had worn in college. It was a most beautiful pink-and-silver ruffled dress and I swooned a lot at seeing it. Well, after they had gone to church, and I had been put to bed while Reesie baby-sat in the living room, I decided to go to church. After all, I was now a grown-up lady. I sneaked into Mother's room, got down the dress by means of a boudoir stool, got down her white hat, her white shoes, her white purse and proceeded to get dressed. I powdered my nose as I had seen Mother do and walked out, the purse clutched tightly under my arm. As I passed Reesie, who was slouched in a chair reading a murder mystery, I said, "Good night Reesie, I'm going to church." Reesie was in such a state of shock, and convulsed with laughter that she didn't stop me. I went to church and let myself in by way of the sanctuary door, which leads on to the pulpit. The topic of Grandfather's sermon was, "Children Follow in Their Parents' Footsteps" so when I entered, I nodded and smiled to Grandfather as I had seen Mother do, and then to the congregation because this is what you do, and as I crossed the floor to take a seat he said, "I've just made a point." Mother, I noticed, had slipped down below the pew.

My Hollywood days were approaching now because I had recently been taken to see a Sonja Henie movie. I can't remember the title, but I certainly recall making up my mind then and there that I was going to Hollywood to be Sonja. The next morning I rose very early, packed my things in my doll suitcase, bid a silent farewell to the sleeping house and tiptoed out. When my parents woke and found me gone they scouted around the house, the yard, but no me. They called the police and soon the entire city was on the lookout for Sweetie/Old Girl/Little Margaret. Hours later, that afternoon, they found me strolling along a street. My parents were ecstatically happy, Mother wept. "Where were you going?" "I'm going to Hollywood to be a movie star." They explained, hugging me all the way home, that one doesn't walk to Hollywood, no, you have to take a plane. I didn't forget that.

Several months went by and Mother was beginning to feel better so we went to visit Nanny for a few days in Asheville. I was happy to go and see familiar faces because I was a very lonely child and seldom had anyone to play with other than Reesie. I longed for a sister or brother to take away the loneliness.

One day in Asheville Mother and I were on our way to the park and as we strolled along I spied a dirty baby playing near the sidewalk. His diaper was wet so I thought, *Oh, that poor little baby needs a mother. He needs to be cleaned and taken care of.* I decided to be his mother. I tried to pick him up but I was too little so I grabbed him by the neck and started dragging him with me. Mother was walking a little ahead of me so she did not know what I was up to. She turned around and saw me. She got very upset and the baby was crying. She pulled my arms loose and said, "Sweetie, whatever are you doing?" I said, "Nobody loves him because he isn't clean so I'm going to take him home and be his mother." She said, "Honey, I promise to do my best to get you a brother or a sister, but we can't take somebody else's brother." That was that. I looked back at the dirty kid and went on to the park.

All of a sudden a couple of trashy-looking women came running up to Mother and one of them grabbed her arm, swinging her around. "You tried to steal my baby!" Mother was terrified and the other one grabbed me. "You tried to take her baby so we're gonna take your little girl!" I remember Mother's terror. She was paralyzed with fear as she tried to explain what had happened. They were yelling and pushing Mother around and just about to beat her up when the commotion brought the superintendent of the park over. They told him what they thought had happened and he believed those women instead of my mother, who couldn't look more like a lady. He warned Mother to leave "and not go stealin' other folks younguns."

Soon after we returned to Winston-Salem, my parents befriended a young girl who had had an illegitimate child. They were trying to help her find her way because she didn't want to lose her daughter. So, for a time, I had a temporary sister in her little girl. We were both four years old but since I identified with Mother, she was a baby to me. I loved her to pieces and she was my all-day companion. But trouble was brewing for the young mother. She tried to work at all sorts of jobs but the state stepped in. Until she could prove better support, the little girl had to go to a children's home.

I shall never forget that horrible day. We all went with her, and the matron or whoever gave us a tour of this place. I wanted to take all those children home with me. Beds all in a row—it was so sad. Big-eyed little faces looked at you and you just wanted to die. Then, I saw the child being taken away screaming and her mother crying. That made an impression on me that took a long time to get over. Until that day, I didn't know that people could take children away from their parents. I lived in constant fear that if anything happened to my parents, I would be put in there.

We lived in Winston-Salem only a year. Maybe they did not like Daddy's brand of medicine or maybe it was another promotion, I don't know, but a few weeks before we were to move to Mount Holly, Reesie came running in the house one day and up the stairs and into Mother's bedroom and jumped in the bed. I charged up after her and she was shivering and crying. I was going to get in bed with her to help her feel better and she shoved me back. "You get out of this bed and out of this house. Don't come near me!" I saw her face was all swollen and bruised and I didn't understand so I started to cry. Mother hurried in, grabbed me, whisked me out of the room and down into the basement. Mother explained to me while we hid down there that Reesie's husband had tried to kill her and was on his way to our house to kill her and us, too. Daddy was in the house with the police, waiting for him. They caught him, but about two weeks after we moved, we learned that poor Reesie killed herself by drinking a bottle of Lysol because after we left there was no one to protect her from that raving maniac of a husband. That also made a permanent impression on me because there was a time after I got married, when I wanted to kill myself to get away from my husband and almost did, had he not stopped me in time.

2

I loved the name of our new town, Mount Holly. It was the halfway mark to *Holly*wood and believe me, their child stars had nothing on me. It was here I gave one of my best performances and told my first whopper. Whether child or adult, no one can live without people of their own generation. My mother played dress up with me, invented games, but still, it did not bridge the generation gap. I had no one my age to talk with and the longing for a brother or sister grew to such greatness that there was no other way for me but to make it come true. I did not forget that babies come from seeds so, one night just before a revival meeting, I worked out my plan, went over the dialogue and proceeded to set the stage.

Our parsonage was right next door to the church so while Mother was getting dressed I marched myself over to the church entrance and, knowing all the church ladies, I greeted each of them, keeping one eye on the lookout for Mother—and Act One was on. I could give you a smile right out of a honeycomb and roll my eyes up at you with such sweetness and light that even Our Father would sigh a sigh. That's what I did. "Oh, good evening, Mrs. Jones, my mother may not be here tonight." "Oh, my dear, what is wrong?" I tilted my head and gave them that heavenly look. "Didn't you know that Mother is going to have a baby? She isn't feeling well." I don't know how I knew at that age that you don't feel well when you're pregnant, but I guess it sounded right to me. May I say that by morning it was all over Mount Holly that Mrs. McLarty was expecting. I was just absolutely positive that it would come true because I thought she would get so embarrassed that she would go out and find a seed and give it to Daddy. She didn't. She never said a word about having that baby. Weeks went by and still, no baby.

I decided since she would not have one—I would. Now, I had gradually made friends with Russell. We were the same age: four and a half. He lived next door and for some reason he preferred playing with boys, but I was a very persuasive child and what could he do actually? He was trapped. He couldn't spend all of his time hiding from me. So, when he sort of got used to me I asked him to marry me. He said yes. I flew in the house all aflutter and asked Mother if it would be all right for Russell and me to marry and she said yes. By this time I had been flower girl at a lot of weddings so I knew a bride had to have a white gown. Mother gave me one of her white satin slips to wear and we got out her ribbon box and I got Russell's cat and put a bow on him and tied him up to the banister on our porch. Mother blew her nose, which was probably an accident, but this is what people do at weddings and the cat cried so that was our ceremony. From that moment on, I introduced anybody and everybody to my husband, Russell. To my mind he was. I was married to him, wasn't I?

It wasn't difficult to figure that if you are married you live together. I told Mother one day that Russell was moving in with us. "Sweetie! Whatever for?" "We're married and we have to sleep together." "Now, Sweetie . . . ?" She tried to explain that there was a difference about fifteen years long between my cat wedding and a real church wedding. Well, couldn't we at least sleep together? No, you couldn't do that either. For once my poor mother was stymied. She found it most difficult to express herself, but she made it very clear that this too was a no-no.

I was going to have that baby no matter what so I went in the kitchen and got a little bowl and went around the neighborhood looking for seeds to give Russell so he could fertilize me. They didn't take. He had a whole pocketful of seeds and not one of them worked. So, I reasoned, with great compassion now for my dear mother, that this might well account for her difficulty in delivering to me a baby brother or sister. Some seeds were just plain rotten.

Disheartened and facing the fact that my marriage was a bore and a failure I decided the time had now come for moving on to greater things. Hollywood. Wanting to do the right thing by Russell I asked him if he wanted to go with me. No. Okay, I had done my duty so I announced that our marriage was ended. He seemed very relieved and overanxious to know how soon I planned on leaving. I informed him the time had arrived. Now.

I went in the house and looked through my wardrobe, choosing what would be appropriate for a star. Most important was Mother's best perfume. A star must always smell good. I told Mother I was leaving and she nodded and went on with her sewing. I packed and then decided to ask Mrs. Pierce, my best friend in all of Mount Holly, who lived across the street. She was a wonderful lady who truly understood me and recognized my talents. She would let me wear all her good clothes and her jewelry and let me faint on her feather comforter a lot (I had seen movies where ladies fainted). I called her and asked if she would like to go to Hollywood with me. I never dreamed she would want to go what with her family to take care of so when she said yes, I nearly died. How would I get her on my tricycle? She said she would have to pack her grip and that was my out. "I'm so sorry, Mrs. Pierce, but I'm in a hurry. Good-bye." Then, I decided to call this girl Ruth, who never believed that I would be a movie star. She said, "Margaret! I do not believe you are going to Hollywood." I said, "Well, I'll call you from the airport and then you'll believe me." I got on my tricycle and rode around the block a few times and went back in the house and called Ruth and made tapping sounds with a pencil near the phone because I had been told they had a lot of typewriters at airports. "Ruth, this is good-bye, dear. I can hardly hear you, dear, for all these typewriters. I'll send you a postcard with my picture on it after I make my first movie. Good-bye." And that was that. As far as I was concerned I was at the airport and on my way. Make-believe was as real as reality for me and most of the children I knew did not understand me and could not play my games. They made mud pies and I made movie sets.

On my fifth birthday I was to have a party and Mother was as excited as I was. That morning I just couldn't wait to open my present from them because, from the weight, I suspected what it was: skates! Something I had desperately wanted. Now, Daddy didn't have much money, but whatever he bought me was always the best. They were magnificent. In my imagination I was zapping all over Mount Holly like a flash. I could go much faster on skates than on a tricycle and there's something about speed, something so exhilarating that you feel sort of indestructible but when I put the skates on they were so heavy I couldn't lift my feet. My heart at that moment was as heavy as those solid steel ball bearings. Mother already had them in her hands, her eyes dancing mischievously. "Sweetie, may I try them on?" That yellow-eyed tiger in me rose up. Jealousy clutched my stomach but I became gallant and generous and gulped, "Yes."

Since Mother didn't want to make a fool of herself in front of all Mount Holly there was only one place to try out the skates. Daddy's church. His study had a nice slick floor so we went to church, my feet feeling heavier than when the skates were on my shoes. I almost hoped she'd fall and . . . no, not really, but just a little. Actually, I was getting sick, but they didn't know it.

We went to Daddy's study and I became part of the furniture and vanished into a corner chair while they had the time of their life. Mother was like a little girl and as she skated around the room, Daddy sang and they laughed, having fun. I got so mad and I already felt sick so I threw up. Mother said, "Ohhh, Sweetie's jealous." I knew she had every reason to think that was what was wrong with me because only a few weeks back I had been plagued with hatred over a purse of hers. She had known for some time I was jealous of it. It was a beautiful maroon suède bag. Her pride and joy. She wore it with matching suède gloves and a rose-colored hat. She looked lovely in that color. But ever since she got that outfit I had grown maroon with jealousy. It was, "Don't put your feet on the purse." Or, "Don't put your hands on the purse." It was so da-dee-da-precious that one day I got so mad at the bag I threw up on it. Poor Mother. I felt awful about doing it, but I couldn't help it. That purse seemed more important than anything in the world to her and I couldn't stand it. I wanted to be the big it. The one at all times. So, Mother guessed since she was having fun with my skates that I was just full of jealousy.

We went home and Mother got me ready for the party but I did not feel well. I did not say anything more because I knew she would think it was the skates. When all the children started to arrive, I forced myself to perk up and, as usual, when I blew out the candles I sang Happy Birthday, Dear Me. The kids thought I was weird, but I didn't care. I loved me. Then, we went out to play and I just lay down on the steps. When Mother saw that she knew I had to be ill. They quickly ended the party and took me to see a Dr. Heart (which I am sure he did not have one of because I was black and blue every day from him). He was very rough on children.

My parents were told I had a streptococcus infection of the ear which later spread to the other ear and to my throat. Every day I had to be taken to this horrible doctor to have my ears lanced. I got worse. Mount Holly has a terrible climate, blistering hot in summer and bitter cold and damp in the winter so between the climate and my condition, I had a tough time recovering. The doctor advised my parents not to put me in the hospital as there was the possibility I would die and under such conditions I would be better off in Mother's care.

I remained bedridden for a year, which isn't easy to take at any age, but when you're five years old you're busting your britches to go, to know, to grow, and time at that age can give you a million hours in a minute. It's paper dolls and a bag full of marbles and going to Hollywood and . . .

My parents prayed, the congregation prayed and for one incredible eternity I lay on my back and wished on the stars I could see at the edge of my window every night. With that many prayers and that many wishes even a Samson couldn't bump me off.

The next year I started school—a year behind everybody else which bothered me terribly. But my real trauma came when I went to meet Mother, who was teaching the second grade. I stood in that doorway and that yellow-eyed tiger had never been more disturbed than at that moment when I saw her being so nice to all those children, taking up her time with all those children and I wanted to kill every one of them. I hated them. I was furious with my mother for sharing herself with them. I didn't know that not only was she sharing herself with them, but she had told them all to come over to our backyard and pick up our bumper crop of pears from the ground.

That afternoon I heard all this commotion and when I looked out in the yard and saw those second-grade monsters I planned to run out and yell, "Ha, ha, you have to pick pears off the ground while I pick them off the trees." Instead, I got so upset I yelled, "Ha, ha, you have to pick the pears off the trees while I pick them off the ground." I was so mad because I didn't get my lines right. It was disgraceful. Because of my jealousy, Mother quit teaching school for a time. She started teaching piano.

This adorable little girl named Ruby Jean started studying with Mother. She had long curls and always looked so pretty when she came for her lessons. I tried to like her and I could have if Mother would have let me sit in on her lessons, but no, that door was closed to me and I was not to disturb them while Ruby Jean was in there. I couldn't stand being left out like that. Why couldn't I watch? A few weeks of struggling with my passionate fury led to an ultimate explosion which was set off when Ruby Jean left her pocketbook one day and Mother wouldn't let me see in it. Not only was I not allowed to watch her take a lesson because she was so special, I wasn't permitted to snoop in her pocketbook! So, the next day as Ruby Jean was coming in the door I said, "Hey, Ruby Jean, how are you?" I acted very friendly and sugary. She sort of shied up to me and said, "Hey, Margaret." With that I drew my hands from behind my back and clonked her over the head with one of Daddy's hard wooden shoe trees. I nearly killed her. Mother quit teaching piano.

In those days, I was very physical in expressing myself. I had not acquired the ability to express my resentments or sentiments verbally. I responded to my feelings by using my body. And the Christmas pageant cost me my astral self.

I was to be an angel in the pageant with the usual wings, halo and wand with a big shiny gold star on top and I was to sing solo, "Come Softly, Tread Gently." But Frances had other ideas. Frances was a little girl who liked me and because I appreciated this fact, I listened to her plea. She begged me to let her sing with me and be an angel, too. Daddy, of course, thought that would be just fine. I didn't think it so fine, but I wanted to be big about it so, okay. When we started rehearsing our number I discovered to my horror Frances couldn't carry a tune. I did not want to go through with this disaster, but I didn't want to hurt her either, so I had to stick to my word.

Opening night came and there we stood. Two dear little angels. We started singing and poor Frances was on a monotone note and I thought, *I bet the audience thinks that's me!* I couldn't bear it any longer. I turned around to her and bopped her over the head with my wand so she'd shut up a minute so they would realize I could sing. Daddy clipped my wings and removed my halo.

I was very theatrically minded as my parents were beginning to see, though they found the price of having a dramatic daughter a bit high. Still, they wanted to help me express myself since they knew they couldn't suppress the actress in me. So Mother, who is very talented herself, decided to write a poem which we would recite for a parents' meeting at church. It was a question-answer poem done in rhyme. I would ask the questions and she would answer. We rehearsed it for days and the grand night came around but when the congregation started with, "Oh, Little Margaret is going to recite a poem for us," and, "Little Margaret is so sweet and so good," I couldn't bear it. I decided I wasn't going to recite anything and I wasn't so sweet and so good and I wished they would stop shoving it down my throat. Mother got up. I was to follow and we were to begin the recital. I ran up there and stood on my head and turned cartwheels and sang and giggled and did everything crazy I could think of but I would not recite that poem. Mother cried. I felt sorry for her but I thought, *She doesn't understand it's because they're making too big a fuss over me.* If they had made a fuss over my talent after I'd done the poem I would have loved them for it but I couldn't stand all that saccharine stuff.

For a few days there was a dark cloud floating around our home but the sunshine poured in when my favorite uncle in all the world came to visit us for a while. Uncle Tokie. He could make anyone smile and he had the same talent for making things grow. Wherever he went, things sprouted and flourished. He had just come back from a city called New York. And what exciting stories he told to me about that wonderful town. He had dark curly hair and gray-green eyes that you could see your face in and a cleft in his chin that fascinated me. I used to sit with a pencil stuck in my chin trying to grow one like his. I loved and adored Uncle Tokie. When he used to come to see us we would play Going to Hollywood. Now we started playing Going to New York. He said it was the most glamorous place in the whole world. Far more exciting than Hollywood. That didn't seem possible, but I knew if Uncle Tokie said it was so, then it was so. He knew everything. Daddy had an electric train set in one of the rooms we didn't use upstairs and Uncle Tokie and I would go up there and pretend to ride the train to New York. I learned a lot about how a lady is supposed to act when she's on a date. He also taught me how to set a fancy table. He got out Mother's beautiful china and crystal and silver and while Mother gasped what appeared to be her last breath, he arranged a table the way it is done in elegant New York restaurants and then let me try it.

His favorite girl friend was Elmira so I used to be Elmira often. One day we were pretending that I lived in New York and he was coming to visit me. When he arrived I said, "Oh, dear Tokie, I am so sorry you came over today because my house is such a mess." And he said you must never say that to anyone because if you say you are sorry they came today it makes it sound as though you don't really want them to come at all. So I learned never to say that and I never have. But more important than anything else, I learned that there was another place where one could be a star. I now had an alternative. If I didn't get to Hollywood, I could go to New York.

Now we had another house guest. Nanny, whom I loved to pieces. She had been ill and had come to stay with us while she recuperated. Having both Uncle Tokie and Nanny was like being back home in Asheville. One day I skipped happily into the house and called to Mother, who usually gave me a "Yoo-hoo, Sweetie, I'm in here." Nanny came out of her room and informed me that my parents had gone to Charlotte for lunch. I went into a rage because they had not told me they were going. I had a picture of them sitting in a beautiful restaurant like the elegant places in New York Uncle Tokie had described, having a wonderful time, laughing and saying, "Ho, ho, she's not here today. We can have a good time."

Being an only child and not having other children to share things with, I naturally drew my parents more and more into the center of my existence. I was possessed by possessiveness. I stood there, looking at my sweet grandmother, and had a first-class tantrum. I told an outlandish lie which she believed because Sweetie couldn't possibly tell a fib. I planted two fisted hands on my skinny hips and staunchly stated, "My parents should be here because something wonderful has happened to me and they should be here." "Well, honey lamb, what is it?" "I have been made the leader of the school band! (I'm in the first grade, remember.) They should be here for such an important event." Poor Nanny, she believed it and was so excited for me. Her enthusiasm didn't take. I was boiling.

Suddenly the phone rang and I started for it but Nanny intercepted me with, "I'd better answer it because it may be your mother." Now I was really incensed. "That's my phone, not yours and I'm answering it." She reached out for me, meaning to embrace me. "Honey lamb, whatever is wrong?" I was all fists and feet and I thought she was attempting to hold me back so I hit out at her, not meaning to, but I wanted to answer that phone. By accident, I kicked her hard in the leg. It stopped her short and she started crying and I started crying and she ran to her room and I ran to mine and nobody answered the phone.

When Mother came home, Nanny told her what I had done.

I was on my bed, crying my heart out because I had been bad and I was ashamed of hurting Nanny, when Mother rushed in. She threw herself over me and I thought she was going to kill me. This was the first time I had ever seen her furious. "How dare you kick *my* mother?" It sounded so strange. I'd never thought of Nanny as *her* mother. "How dare you kick her? You deserve to be shot alone!" This so terrified me I expected any minute to be taken out in the yard and shot the way I had seen people shot in the movies. She jumped up, crying, and ran out of the room and locked me in. What she actually said was, "You should be shut up alone." I didn't get that straight until about twenty years later so for most of my life I thought she had wanted to kill me that day.

About three hours later she came in and ordered me out in the yard. Again, she locked me out. I screamed and yelled and pounded on the door and nobody paid any attention. When my daddy came home, she told him to leave me out there. When he wouldn't let me in I realized all was lost. I would be left outside until they found a policeman who would come and when they said, "Fire," he would shoot and I'd be dead.

I wandered around the yard, sobbing and thinking. How could I make them love me again? I looked at the once white house which badly needed a coat of paint and I thought that if I washed it and got all that dirt off, it would be beautiful and they would love me again. I got a bucket and found an old rag and filled up the bucket and went to work. I made the most beautiful white spot on one wall. I was only three feet tall so my work was limited. Daddy came out and I proudly displayed my artwork. He hugged me and picked me up, explaining that a Methodist parsonage was not completely your own and that we had no right to make repairs without the consent of the church committee, so we got dirt and smeared it over the white spot until it matched the rest of the house.

I never mentioned my execution because I thought they had forgotten and, if I reminded them, they would carry out the order instantly. I realized that I must never again get happy because they might, at any moment, remember to have me shot. I vowed to be very good so they wouldn't think about it. But I couldn't understand how they could change like that. All kinds of wonderful memories came back to me like the summer before when we were at the beach. One day we were picking up shells and Mother walked off in one direction and Daddy in another and I thought they were leaving me. I let out a scream and Mother turned and realized Daddy wasn't with me and he looked back and they both came running toward me, their arms outstretched. I felt really loved that day. Mother had looked so beautiful in her red bathing suit with her long dark hair falling about her shoulders and she had a lovely figure. And Daddy, all grins and muscle. I couldn't understand how they could love me so much and then want to have me killed.

One day when Daddy drove me to school, we passed the police station and I ducked down to the floor. He said, "Old Girl, what are you doing on the floor? You act like you have a guilt complex." And I couldn't tell him because he might say, "Oh, good, there's a policeman. I'll have you shot now."

One night I woke up to the sound of fire engines. Blue smoke was churning and twisting all around me and I yelled and nobody came. I was too terrified to get out of the bed and then Uncle Tokie appeared and picked me up, taking me outside. In the living room a bunch of firemen were collected and Mother was serving coffee to everybody. One whole wall in the living room was a charred mess and water dripped all over the place. I learned later my daddy put the fire out himself, but the firemen came to make sure the house was safe. When Uncle Tokie took me in the dining room where Mother was busy making coffee I saw all her silver out on the table and I said, very meekly, "Mother? Were you going to save me after you saved your silver?" She cried.

After that, I had a phobia of fire. I wouldn't wear anything orange, red or yellow. I wouldn't even use the word fire. When I heard anyone talk about a fire I got violently ill and threw up. Right after this episode, we moved to Boone, named after Daniel. There were forest fires there constantly which only fed the flame of my fear, but aside from that, it was the most beautiful country we ever lived in.

Boone is high in the Appalachian Mountains. Very rugged country and very beautiful. The hottest day never went over the seventies. The air was so pure you wanted to eat it. We had the most exquisite garden we'd ever had because in that climate absolutely anything would grow. Mother and I had the most wonderful time growing flowers. I still had my wand from that fatal day I cracked Frances over the head and I used my wand to put the flowers to sleep each night. Mother and I played make-believe with them all the time. We would sing songs to them and fun things like that. One evening I was dancing around the garden, dubbing each flower a pleasant snooze when I looked up at that fantastic sky that was so close you felt you could reach up and pluck the stars and I saw a luminous ring around the moon. I made a wish on it. I said, "Moon light, moon bright, the beautiful moon of tonight, I wish I may, I wish I might have the wish I wish tonight. Make me a movie star." I knew it would come true.

The next morning I got up and packed and waited. I told Mother somebody was coming to take me to Hollywood or New York and, as usual, she nodded and went on about her work. I waited all day. I told my neighbors good-bye. Nobody came. I got mad and decided I would make it come true if it took the rest of my life. Even then I was beginning to know that you can have what you want if you want it badly enough.

It was in Boone that I had my first formal birthday party. I loved formal clothes because that was like being an actress. Mother had the same weakness. One day we were in town shopping and I spied this beautiful pastel yellow dress with white polka dots and I died for it. It was so magnificent and Mother loved it as much as I did. It was nine dollars—a lot of money, but she couldn't resist. Well, I had the dress—now what? That's when we decided to have a formal birthday party. Then, at least, we wouldn't have to feel so guilty about our extravagance.

On my eighth birthday I had a glorious party with all girls. I loved boys but I was afraid they would chase us and spoil our beautiful dresses. The party didn't quite make it because even when you are only eight years old boys are nice to have around.

Mickey, the cocker spaniel, as I've said, was my most loving companion. She just sort of followed me around wherever I went, but she wasn't allowed to leave the yard. She was right behind me so long as I was in or around the house, but one day she met some ugly old mutt and she got her tail stuck against his tail and she was whimpering and Mother was raging. I said, "What is Mickey staying with that old dog for if she doesn't like him?" Mother explained that Mickey for some unknown reason had given that mongrel a seed and he was fertilizing her. She ran in the house as I watched, crying because Mickey was crying and Mother came running out with a bucket of water and threw it on them. Well, that's what you do when you put a seed in the ground, you give it water so I thought that is the way fertilizing dogs works, too. I was sorry to see Mickey unhappy about the coming baby, but I was thrilled to think I would have another just like her to play with. Mother didn't seem overjoyed. On the contrary, she was yelling, "Git!" to that other dog and Mickey's tail was now between her legs and she was "gittin'," too.

Mother grabbed Mickey and threw her in the basement, all wet, and wouldn't let her come out. I could not understand why she was being punished for having a baby. Now, the whole idea was becoming more than confusing and I was glad that Russell's seeds didn't take that time when I went around looking for seeds so he could fertilize me. Mickey got distemper from being left wet and in that cold, damp basement. The next day she was really sick so we took her to a country vet. I was never so miserable as the day I had to leave her there. I asked Mother why she had punished Mickey and she said, very arrogantly, "Mickey knows better than to mix with common dogs. She knows she's a thoroughbred."

Poor Mickey was near death for three weeks, the doctor said, and finally he called and suggested we take her home as the danger had passed and he thought she would pull through. We did, but the next day Mother and I were going to Asheville to visit Nanny so Mother thought Mickey would be better off at the vet's because Daddy was so busy at the church. When Mickey saw us leave her at the vet's she just lay down and died. We didn't know it then, but Daddy sent us a special delivery letter in Asheville telling us she was gone. The vet said she died of a broken heart because she thought we were abandoning her. I was in the yard playing "nurse" and Mother had found an old pair of white stockings at Nanny's and I was wearing them and when she came out and told me Mickey was gone, I started screaming and running and the stockings fell down and I tripped over them and yanked them off and climbed up a tree and cried all day. I stayed up there until supper and would not come down.

When we came home we went to see the vet and he told me Mickey was the sweetest dog he had ever known and that he had come to love her so much that he buried her beneath his favorite lilac bush and he showed it to me. When I lost her, I lost something of myself.

We lived in Boone a year. That fall, just before the conference, Mother made baked squash (fresh from the garden) and she made a lot of it. On the third day of having it, as she passed the plate to Daddy he said, "No, thank you." I thought, *If he says no, then I say no. I'm Daddy's girl.* Mother offered the plate to me. "No, thank you." She glared at me and she glared at Daddy and then she whipped around making a lot of "ohh" noises and flew to the kitchen, threw open the back door and sailed plate and all halfway down the mountain. She had spunk and, boy, was she furious.

I am sure I inherited my mother's sensitivity because she truly takes things to heart. When Daddy announced that we were moving to Belmont we were miserable. We all loved Boone, but there is nothing you can do except accept. So, the day before we were to leave, Mother got in the car and drove all over Boone crying and nodding good-bye to it and when she came home, she was crying so hard she didn't notice the garage doors and crashed right through them.

Shortly after we moved to Belmont, Mother and I were in town and I saw a huge paper doll that I wanted desperately (yes, I was eight years old!). It cost one dollar and Mother could not afford to splurge on something like that. She said she would save for it and get it as soon as she could. I had such a strong imagination that I just pretended to have the doll and I played with it, talked to it and finally when Mother bought it, I was tired of it.

A few months after being in Belmont, I finally made a good friend. Dolores. She was very theatrical so we understood each other—or I thought we did. We were always putting on shows for the children in the neighborhood and one day I went to her house and two of her cousins were visiting her. It was on this eventful day that I discovered your best friend isn't always.

One of her cousins had the meanest face you've ever seen. An ugly pinched expression and I thought, *Poor thing, she must be terribly unhappy to have such a mean face. I'll be extra special nice to her.* I tried to talk to her about pleasant things and tried very hard to entertain her, but I could not crack that stone face. The three of us were walking along when she said, "Dolores, let's take Margaret to the bridge and throw her off." The bridge was just ahead and I was terrified, but I had no intention of letting them know it so I walked toward the bridge as they caught me on both sides, the third girl shoving me from the rear.

The bridge ran over an eight-track railroad line and it was quite high. I just went limp and pretended it was all a very funny joke because I was *not* going to show fear. We were on the bridge now and they were dragging me to the edge, to the railing and as they lifted me up I said, "Dolores, you're my friend. You're not supposed to do this." She giggled and said, "Well, they're my cousins and you know blood is thicker than water." I said, yanking a hand free, "You really are going to throw me off the bridge?" "Yeah." "Well, I hate to do this," and I pinched her nose, digging my nails in and she screamed and they dropped me as she jumped back. I started running and as I came off the bridge a man grabbed me and said, "Little girl, don't you know you shouldn't play on the bridge?" I wasn't crying because I didn't want the girls to know how scared and how hurt I was. After meeting the man I pulled myself together and strolled along toward home as though being thrown off a bridge was an everyday occurrence. The girls marched along beside me, chiding me, but I never let my feelings show and when I got home I ran inside and cried and collapsed. I was sick in bed for three days. When I got well I got mad and scratched Dolores off my list.

After my disillusionment over my friend Dolores, I was without anyone I could play with and trust. That's how I got Blackie. She was a beautiful black kitten and I adored her but not in the same way I had loved Mickey. No, that part of me was reserved for her, but I had a lot of fun with Blackie and I would dress her up in doll clothes and put her in my baby carriage and push her around the neighborhood. She loved it, all cozy under the covers and she would stay in the bonnet and dress and diaper just like a real baby. One day she was threatened by a dog who smelled her out and jumped up on the baby carriage. Blackie shot out of there like a streak and a lady passing by dropped her packages and seemed to fall into a state of catatonia as Blackie, in her baby clothes, ran up a tree. I guess the lady thought my doll had come to life.

Blackie was the queen cat of the neighborhood and when she decided to get herself fertilized, that was some sight. She would sit in the yard, head held high, that black coat gleaming like some fine lady of royalty while all these tomcats circled around her as she held court. She picked the ugliest, toughest of them all to be her king. Puddin' Head was his name and he had an ear missing from one of his heroic battles.

One night I had a dream which disturbed me so that it woke me. I dreamed I saw a basket left on the doorstep with one gray kitten in it. When I woke, I ran out to the kitchen where Blackie was and there next to her was one gray kitten. Poor Blackie was in agony. She was having trouble with the babies. I guess she had used her powers of ESP and sent me the message to get up and get help. I woke Mother but Mother didn't know what to do and Daddy was away. The babies didn't come and Mother took Blackie to the vet. That night he called and said if she wanted to save Blackie there was an operation which would cost fifteen dollars and she had a fifty-fifty chance to survive. Mother said she didn't have the money (and she really didn't) and to "go ahead, then." I knew! I knew what that meant and I started screaming and crying. He put Blackie to sleep.

Mother was determined to save the kitten. She asked the vet what she had to do and she did it. Right around the clock for two weeks. Every three hours she would get up and give it milk with an eyedropper and the vitamins and everything. She said, "If this little thing pulls through, I think we should name him Toughy." He pulled through and he was the toughest cat you've ever seen.

Poor Toughy was doomed, too. Mother had him altered so he could not fertilize any cats and to keep him close to home. The vet somehow cut something he shouldn't have and Toughy's hind legs were permanently paralyzed. Well, I was determined to make him the highest jumping cat in Belmont and I did. I taught him how to jump over the fence. Those front legs became so powerful he could do anything with two that other cats did with four, but then, a horrible mean woman next door to us killed him one day when he jumped over the fence. She fed him poison. So, that was my last pet. It seemed everything and everyone I loved always died.

I shared my mother's love of opera. I was raised on it and Aïda became my favorite. I was now taking piano lessons so I memorized all the melody lines and decided I would do the opera for my class. When I had invented a language to my satisfaction, I asked the teacher if I could do the opera for the class. She thought it a pretty funny idea so she said yes. The kids loved it. When they asked me what language it was I said, "Italian," and they believed it and thought I was so smart to know how to speak a foreign language. It was such a success that I asked the teacher if we could put on the opera for the whole school. Because the children were so enthusiastic she agreed.

Since Aïda is the star, I naturally intended to be Aïda, but the girl whose mother was going to supply all the old clothes had other ideas. She intended to be Aïda. Okay, I changed everything around and made Amneris the lead. I had more cool for a kid. I had the boys wearing dresses, and boys at that age . . . but as they moaned I explained that in those days men dressed that way.

We did the show for the entire school in the auditorium. The teachers were hysterical and the kids loved it. I was a smashing success.

It was during this time I began to write opera stories and attempted to set them to music because I was in love. His name was Jerry Johnson, but as in adult life, so often the one we worship has another idol. I was in love with Jerry and Jerry was in love with somebody else and Jimmy Wilson was in love with me.

Right after *Aïda* Jimmy was so taken with me he got the hiccups every time I spoke to him. Mother's favorite story is my first date. With Jimmy. When he came to take me to a Saturday afternoon movie he said, "I've come to get my woman." After the movie we came home and played marbles. I beat him. Later, I beat him up. Mother called me a bully.

One day, shortly after the fight, she was looking for me for something and she saw Jimmy and she asked him if he had seen me. She said he started screaming and fell into a puddle yelling, "Margaret, Margaret," kicking his feet in the air. Poor Jimmy, he had it bad. I continued to dream of Jerry and wrote tons of king and queen stories about us. Some of the music wasn't really bad. In fact, when I first met the composer Lamar Stringfield I showed him some of my music and he insisted I had great talent. And years later, when I was in college, he wanted to manage me and bring me to New York.

By the time I was eleven, I was truly star struck and, having read *Gone With the Wind*, I began to live the life of Scarlett. I persuaded a friend to have a formal dinner party (because I wanted to dress up like Scarlett). Naturally, the first boy I ever kissed in my life over a thrilling game of post office became my Rhett. He also became hostile because boys are not so hot on post office at that age. I lost my Rhett.

Belmont was really the first place where we ever had a beautiful house. The church committee had put their Bible bonnets together and decided to renovate our parsonage. Alas, two weeks after it was completed, we moved. Daddy had become a chaplain in the Navy.

Staten Island was the jumping-off place for that great and wonderful world of New York City. My dream, which Uncle Tokie had fostered, was at last going to come true. It was happiness in capital letters. And Mother had a friend in New York,

Emily Kalter, who was an opera singer with the San Carlos Opera Company and City Center. The first time we went to see her she was in *La Traviata* and after the performance, while everyone was crowding around Emily I sneaked away and went to the now empty stage and stood, stage center, and sang to the dark theater. Mother found me and as she took my hand and led me off I said, "Someday, you'll see—I'm going to be a star."

The next day she gave me a lecture. "Sweetie, the crown must come off. You have got to stop living in a dream world. You have got to face reality." I died. I couldn't understand how *she* couldn't understand that this was what I wanted and nothing else would ever be right for me. I thought, *I can never take off the crown, but from now on I just won't let you know I'm wearing it.*

There had never been a time I did not long for the stage. Even as an infant I loved to pose for pictures. I was fascinated to see my image miraculously reproduced on a piece of paper. Without coaxing, Sweetie/Old Girl/Little Margaret would give you her best profile, her biggest smile, but after that lecture, I never again said aloud "I want to be a star." Not until the day I graduated from college.

That summer we met a friend of my dad's, a Dr. Victor Berger, who was superintendent of schools on Staten Island and who understood my hunger for the arts. It was Dr. Berger who arranged it so I could go to P.S. 45 because they had a drama department, instead of to the school in my vicinity. He told me not to let anyone in my neighborhood know where I went to school as it was against regulations to do what he had done for me. I never did. The kids on the block thought I was cracked when I would say I didn't know the name of my school. "It's private." That's all I would say.

Daddy, not realizing it, gave me my first acting lesson. I was in the fifth grade and had to learn the Preamble to the Constitution of the United States and I just could not seem to learn it. He said, "Old Girl, now just think what you're saying. What does this line mean . . . ?" and he took it apart bit by bit. Suddenly it became an acting piece and I had no trouble with it. The next day all the other kids stumbled over the big words but, to me, every word had been explained so I knew what it meant. Know what you are saying—this is what acting is all about.

One evening Daddy took me with him to visit a minister. He took me to the church and left me in a room where some children were rehearsing a play. What they were doing was all wrong and something inside me rebelled. I had never had an acting lesson, but I knew instinctively that acting is life and you don't do anything unnatural so I said, "May I interrupt a minute?" They were more than happy to hear what I had to say and I explained how the scene should go. You reason things out—that's what it's all about. They tried it and the scene worked and I was very pleased with myself. Not in an egotistical way, but right is right. For me, it was another confirmation. I belonged on the stage.

At P.S. 45 I met a black girl, Audrey. She was a beautiful little girl and we became fast friends and she took me home to meet her family. I adored her mother and thought she was so lovely. That summer, I went to Asheville to visit my grandmother and one day I told her about my friend Audrey and how pretty she was and how beautiful her mother was and what a nice lady . . . Nanny had a fit. "Oh, good grief! You never call a colored woman a lady." "Why can't I call her a lady? She speaks beautifully, she dresses beautifully, she has good taste, she's proper. Why can't I call her a lady?" We had a big fight and I got so uptight I screamed at Nanny and yanked the tablecloth off the table upsetting everything because she wasn't being fair. I could not understand her attitude. That was my first experience, but not my last, as to how some white people think about the blacks. My visit was very brief.

The next year was for me the happiest because Mother was finally going to have a baby. Jimmy was on his way. Mother was having a tough time keeping him and had to go to the hospital because it looked like she might have a miscarriage. After a few days, the danger passed and she seemed to be all right, but since Daddy was being shipped out soon, Mother decided we had better go to Asheville until the baby came.

I was now in the sixth grade and I was going into a new school midterm, which is not easy because school systems are so different, but I was accustomed to moving around by now. When I saw the classroom I was to be assigned to, I was ecstatically happy. The teacher's name was Mrs. Minerva and her room was full of wonderful posters and flowers. She was a very artistic teacher and as long as there was art and beauty I was home. I couldn't wait to start. I knew I would get my period very soon and I wasn't afraid anymore because I thought a lady like Mrs. Minerva would take care of me. She certainly did that. She turned out to be a Communist!

One day she wrote *U.S.S.R.* on the blackboard and said, "Now, this is very like the U.S.A., but the U.S.S.R. is better because they have an idealistic social system where everyone shares everything with each other. There are no poor people and no filthy rich people." Well, I'd never been filthy rich in my life, I was a poor little church mouse, but I took great exception to this because my parents had taught me to respect people who were able to accomplish things on their own. A purple-eyed dragon was wrestling inside me. She went on, "It's such a wonderful way to live because no one needs to suffer. If you have a thriving farm on one side of the road and there are people living on the other side of the road who are starving, you will give them half of what you have and then no one will be hungry." All the children nodded, thinking what a nice way to live this was. I couldn't stand it. "But what if I worked very hard to raise my crops and the people across from me were lazy? Why should I give them half of what I worked so hard for? No sir! Nobody's going to take my food away from me!"

She knew I would never go for her "philosophy" and she began making fun of me at every opportunity. From that moment on, she made my life a hell. She made fun of my singing for one thing and I was already writing music which was considered quite good by the music teacher. We had a special music teacher who came in to teach us and she came around to all the classes and said I was very good as a student and as a composer. A few weeks after I sassed Mrs. Minerva, there was to be a song contest. All the students were to write a song and submit it. I won. Mrs. Minerva could have killed me for winning. It was the old straw story but Mrs. Minerva was no gentle camel. She was an artistic murderer.

One afternoon, when I got up to sing a song, as everyone had to do, she stood behind me and stopped up her ears and laughed and mocked me. Of course, the whole class did the same because they all loved Mrs. Minerva. She was a horrible, destructive woman.

She hated me, she hated a boy named Clyde, who was also artistic, Clyde Griggsby. He wrote beautiful music and could paint and she hated another girl, Nonnie Steedman, who was also very talented and very musical. Later in college, Nonnie was my roommate, but Mrs. Minerva apparently hated any child who seemed to be outstanding creatively. We learned later that Mrs. Minerva had a son who turned out not to be as artistic as she had hoped so I guess she was getting her revenge on others.

Because of her I became afraid to sing, afraid to act, afraid to appear in front of people, and it took me years to overcome this. She also twisted everything I said.

The day Jimmy was born, they called me at school to tell me I had a baby brother and I ran back into the room all excited and yelled, "I'm a brother." She made me stay in after school because I made myself so obscene by calling myself a brother. When Jimmy was born my daddy came home to be with us for a while.

He was to take me on a little trip somewhere which would keep me out of school a day and a half. The principal had given me permission so everything was set for my leaving. In the meantime I got deathly ill over the weekend and we couldn't go. The next Monday I had a fever of 102 but Daddy didn't want me to miss school and neither did I, so I went, but I was to go with him to the doctor at eleven, which Mrs. Minerva knew about. All that morning she kept picking on me about being sick. "Little Margaret's daddy comes back from the Navy and she has to go away on a trip. Isn't that nice? Now she claims she's sick and has to get out at eleven to see the doctor. We don't believe she's sick, do we, class?"

I saw Daddy's car pull up in front of the school and I told her. She pretended not to hear me and wouldn't let me leave. My daddy came in, looking very handsome in his uniform and he said, "Come on, Margaret, we're going to be late." She purred at him. "Why, Lieutenant McLarty! All Little Margaret had to say was that you were here—" Of course I had said it and she knew perfectly well he was out front. I hated her guts. She was a real demon and I hope she reads this book. I've hated her all my life because she started my fears, which I had never known about before I met her.

When graduation came around, she wouldn't let me be in the program—or Clyde, or Nonnie. She made us stay in the room while the commencement exercises were going on. Our parents wondered where in the world we were and they were quite upset, but she had planted such fear in us that she made us come back after graduation and clean up her room. When I got home Mother wanted to know where we had been and I told her. She was furious and when I said I had to go back now and clean up the room she said, "Why? School is out and you most certainly do not have to clean up her room or any room in that school!" "Yes, I have to." I went. I was absolutely intimidated by this horrible woman. Clyde and Nonnie came in and we were straightening up all the mess and suddenly I said, "Clyde, why are we here?" He said, "Mrs. Minerva said we had to clean up this room." "What can she do to us now? We're no longer connected with this school." He said, "That's right. We're not. We go to junior high now. Let's go."

3

hen my daddy got out of the Navy, we moved back to Staten Island for a short time and he took over a church for a minister who was ill. As soon as the man regained his health he returned to his flock and Daddy was given a church in Marion, back in North Carolina.

The church in Marion was some distance away from our new home and our new home was quite different from the modest and usually livable parsonages I had grown up in. This was a big, ugly old house and badly needed a lot more than paint. Now that I look back on it, I realize it had many distinguished features but I could not appreciate them at the age of thirteen. The woodwork was beautiful; a slender, handsome spiral staircase dominated the enormous hall. The ceilings were sky high and the floors were of deep mahogany. Even though I was told this Victorian house had once been the center of attraction in all of Marion, owned by a young, vital, brilliant and rich man, it still stood there like some old horror movie setting. I expected Bela Lugosi to say I was sleeping in his bed or to find the Headless Horseman galloping through the long hall, which I called a breezeway, and which ran the full length of the house. I was scared out of my mind to live in that house. So, that first day, I stood on the veranda and cried. I looked over the banister as a rustling sound caught my attention and there racing out from under the house were two huge rats! That helped a lot. Not only would I find Bela but the Pied Piper and all the rats that hadn't gone over the edge. We moved in despite my hysteria and Sweetie/Old Girl was given a lot of "there, there" and a lovely story that was supposed to make me feel much better. It didn't. The story only puffed up my imagination and made life more unbearable.

I was told that the man who had once lived in this house had built it for his young and beautiful bride. She died during pregnancy. She was to have had twins and something went wrong so they died. He gave up his business, his life, and vanished. Years later his body was found in a lean-to. He had become a tramp and had been keeping somebody's pigs. Now, of course, I had his ghost and his beloved wife to think about.

My handy daddy fixed up the place as best he could and we didn't use any of the rooms upstairs. When I started to school, every day I would walk along with the kids, right past my house, go up to the corner, turn and wave good-bye to them and then when everyone was gone I would go around to the back lot behind our house and climb up the lot and enter the house from the back door. First of all, I'm sure the children thought I was nuts because the whole town certainly knew where the Methodist minister lived, but I was ashamed of the house. I felt so poor. I'm not saying there's anything wrong with being poor, but I had never lived in a house like that. Actually, I think Mother loved it, but as I said, I was too young to appreciate its remaining beauty.

One day Mother saw me coming up the back lot, my books slung over my shoulder and she yelled, "Sweetie, what are you doing out there with all those rats?" I came in the house and said, "I don't want anyone to know where I live. I'm ashamed to walk up to the front door." Mother cried.

I really worked on liking the house because I realized I had no choice and I might as well make the most of it. After a few weeks of brainwashing myself, with the help of my ready imagination, I came to like it. It became a Southern plantation and I would go upstairs when I came home from school, and act out the days of Scarlett O'Hara. I had a lot of evening dresses, some Mother's, some she had made for me, and I would put one on and pretend to entertain a room full of distinguished ladies and gentlemen. Grandfather McLarty had retired and was away on his second honeymoon. He had left his exquisite china (some of it was Dresden) and silver and crystal in our care. It was boxed and stored in several of the rooms up there. (That was a funny wedding. My own father marrying his father to our very dear Aunt Jane.) I would take out the silver and all and use it for my make-believe guests. I found out to my dismay, when I finally got to know the girls at school well enough to invite them over to play my game, they thought I was crazy at my age to want to play make-believe. All they wanted to do was paint their nails and talk about boys. I liked boys, too, but I would invite them over and put them into these romantic situations and they usually stopped liking me after our first "tea." But, I finally found a friend who really understood me.

Elizabeth Cross was a beautiful child. She had long brown hair and enormous brown eyes and a face that any artist would wish to paint. She was an extraordinary child; her imagination contested mine, and her ability as a horsewoman left me dazzled in awe because this child was only nine years old and all the girls at school made fun of me for having her as my friend. I didn't care. She was my dearest friend the whole four years I lived there.

Elizabeth was an only child. She was lonely just as I was so we became inseparable. She lived in the most gorgeous house I had ever seen, swarming with many servants. Her greatest love was horses and she taught me to ride. Even then, she was quite well known for her horsemanship and before she died, she won the Madison Square Garden world championship for five-gaited ponies.

I practically lived at her house because she was such fun to be with and her parents were often busy so she welcomed my visits. One day we were playing a game of saving some poor innocent Indians from marauders and she said, "Let's take out my pony and we'll chase down the bad men." Her pony was one of the world champions and he was all rigged up in a tail set for a coming horse show. I said, "Elizabeth, he's got his tail set on. We can't take that off." She said, "Oh, I know how to take it off and when we're through with our game, I'll put it back on." After the chase, we came back and the groom was still away somewhere so he didn't know what we had done and she could not get that tail set on so, in despair and knowing her parents would be furious, she hung up the tail set and we went in the house for dinner.

Here we were, the two of us in this huge dining room. Elizabeth sat way down at the other end of the table, looking very teeny tiny and she bowed her head for the blessing. She said, "God is great, God is good, let us thank Him for our food and dear God, please get me and Margaret out of this terrible mess— I love you, Elizabeth." My heart just poured out of my eyes and I cried all over the food. He didn't get us out of it and we had hell to pay from her parents. We both got it. Me for letting her and Elizabeth for doing it. She lost the ribbon for that show.

A lot of the girls at school would say, "You're stupid! You shouldn't have her as your friend. She's so much younger than you are. You just like her for her money!" It would make me so mad I could kill them. I liked Elizabeth for herself. She was alive. She was bright and her imagination was fantastic. I adored her. She was my baby sister. I remember one time she came to my house and I had a lot of costume jewelry that my aunts had given me and she put her arms around the jewel box and she said, "Oh, Margaret, it must be wonderful to be a preacher's daughter. I wish I were a preacher's daughter. It must be such fun." It seemed incredible that she would want to be anyone else's daughter. Her parents adored her, as she them. I think it was more that I lived in such an imaginary world and she loved the games I introduced her to. Because she was one child who was never neglected.

Elizabeth asked if I would be a ribbon girl for the horse shows and I proudly said I would. Marion in those days was famous in the South for its fine horse shows, but after Elizabeth was killed, the Cross family stopped showing horses. But, one night, I was at a show, not as a ribbon girl, just there to watch Elizabeth, and she introduced me to the mother of a friend of hers. This lady was the most dramatic person I'd ever met. She had a drink in her hand and a lot of men sat around her. She was very sad looking and everybody seemed in awe of her so I thought, *I'm going to be just like her the next time I am a ribbon girl.*

A few nights later Elizabeth invited me to the show and I decided I would practice dressing up like that lady, so I put on a rose satin gown I often played dress up in, piled my hair up on top of my head, got out my green ballet slippers and sewed green ribbon on them to make straps because that lady had worn shoes with straps, put on this gorgeous long blue coat Elizabeth had bought for me (which hardly went with the dress, but I thought it did), used some of Mother's lipstick, and when my parents came home from church to pick me up for the horse show, it was dark and they didn't notice how I looked.

When I got there, Mother took one look at me as I got out of the car and nearly fainted. "Sweetie! What are you trying to prove?" I thought I looked elegant. Daddy drove off while Mother fanned herself. I sat in Elizabeth's box and nobody would sit with me. She did not say a word about the way I looked, but people kept staring at me and the sad expression I had seen on the lady's face became easier and easier to duplicate. Nobody would sit with me and nobody would talk to me, except Elizabeth. She didn't care what I looked like—she loved me. Of course, I began to get the message that I was a little out of character. I didn't wear that outfit again.

I gave my first dinner party a few weeks later. I had a big crush on Elizabeth's cousin, Gene. He was so handsome that I would absolutely crumble when he looked at me. He had jet black hair and brown eyes and beautiful white teeth and dimples. I was in love. Naturally, the whole purpose of the party was to make him fall in love with me. I invited another couple: Mary Olive and her boy friend. I dressed up like Martha Washington because I had the costume and I thought he would see how grown-up I really was. I powdered my hair and when they got there Gene's eyes fell out—not in the way I had hoped. He was blind to my very existence after that. Nobody ate because they were all so worried that I had aged so much. Mary Olive didn't eat because her family believed you should eat before you go out because you never know what you might get for dinner. The party was a smashing failure. I lost Gene. Things got worse.

I was very dramatic at this time and had seen a movie where the hero saved a girl who was skiing and had fallen down a mountain. The hero looked just like Bill Smith—a boy who had liked me for a long time. So, after seeing the film, Bill became my hero. One day I saw Bill on his bike so I jumped on mine and went racing after him. I was cycling real fast to keep up with him and we were talking but he was being cool and suddenly Patsy Landers came up on her bicycle and sighed, "Hey, Bill," and swished away and he took off after her. I fell off my bike and pretended to faint. I lay there and cried but he didn't turn back and somebody came up and said, "You know, you really shouldn't put on such an act. It won't get you Bill." And I dramatically sobbed, "These are real tears!"

Daddy called Bible School Vacation Church School because we did so many other things besides study the Bible. One day we had a picnic and each of us was to represent some Biblical character we liked. We had to dress like the person and our lunch was to be something like what the people ate in that particular period. I chose to be Esther. She was my heroine. I tried to find a boy to be my king—no luck. Then, I asked Gretchen. She looked almost like a boy because she had broken her neck and her hair was all cut off. She said she would do it and that she would fix our picnic. That day she handed me my sandwich. "Here, Margaret, here's your sandwich." I screamed. There, between two pieces of bread were sardines with their tails hanging out and those eyes staring up at me. She ate hers, tails and all.

Gretchen became a good friend because nobody else understood her. She was very Bohemian and almost as dramatic as I. She told tremendous lies about herself just to get attention. I remember one day, sitting in the balcony of the auditorium, I heard a lot of whispering going on and it finally got to me that

Gretchen was pregnant. She had made it up just to have people talk about her. Poor Gretchen. She also drank. Her parents left her alone a great deal and she would get into the liquor cabinet and get stoned. One night my mother saw her staggering around on the street and she took her home. When Mother came back, all upset about Gretchen, I told her about the rumor and thought how it just might be the truth. Mother said, "Well, if ever Gretchen needed a friend, I guess she needs one now." So, even though none of the other girls would speak to her, I remained her friend.

A few days after her hangover, she called me to come to her house and listen to opera. I loved opera more than anything so I went and she started conducting and she said, "Conduct this for me." I started beating time and she shouted, "That's not the way! You have to throw your head back and put your heart and soul in it. You'll never be a conductor!" We got in the worst fist fight and I didn't speak to her for a whole year. She never had the baby because she was never pregnant but one time I went to see her when we were over our mad and the maid answered the door, whispering, "You better be going. You can't see Miss Gretchen now." "Why? Is she sick?" "Ohh, she's getting it from her mama. She got caught having a smoking party and they're gonna send her away." I guess smoking plain cigarettes in those days would be like getting caught smoking pot today. She probably did that too and ate morning-glory seeds!

They sent Gretchen to a Catholic school and I heard some months later they threw her out because she told the mother superior what she could do to herself. I admired her so. She got kicked out of a lot of schools, but she was very popular wherever she went because she had spunk.

We had a high time that year in the eighth grade because we were almost always without a teacher. There were fifty of us and out of that half a hundred, half of them were holy terrors. We had five teachers in a row. They quit after one day. The principal thought since I was the preacher's daughter I would be the likely one to pick out all the rotten apples and split them up so that chaos could be returned to order. I was to divide us into five sections and proceeded to fulfill my duty with great enthusiasm. I was Miss It, which I loved.

This tough little girl with several teeth knocked out said, "I want to be with Mary Olive." I said, "You can't be. I've already put you in another group." So she prissed all over herself and whined, "Little Miss Margaret, bip, bip, bip. Thinks she's so important." And she kept being so fresh to me and no one had ever done that before and I wanted to smack her and knock out a few more teeth. She was much bigger than I, but I wanted to kill her and then I thought, *No, I'll be little and faint and then all the boys will come to my rescue*, so I did. In all these movies when people talked mean to a lady she fainted so I pretended to faint. But first I said, "What did you say?" She repeated her smart remark and I said, "Ohhhh," and fell to the floor. Everybody stood around and said, "Is she dead?" "I don't know. Kick her and see." Nobody saved me so I got up. One girl, Eva, who liked me and understood my weird ways said, "Margaret? Did you really faint?" I told her I most certainly did and I swayed and caught onto the teacher's desk and gasped, "I think I'm going to faint again. . . ." Eva caught me and yelled at the kids, "You shouldn't talk to Margaret that way. She's too much of a lady," and she cried and I fell to the floor. The girls carried me out and the boys just stood around and smoked.

I didn't bother with the other kids anymore because after that day it had been made quite clear how disliked I was. The minister's daughter. Miss Goody-Goody. There was a lot of name-calling in those days. If they saw me coming down the street they would scatter or deliberately wait until I got close enough to hear them and they would say, "Here comes the *minister's daughter*, Miss Priss Margaret!" and run. The only people who liked me were the parents of these little monsters, which only made them dislike me all the more. Young people can be terribly cruel, but no matter how hurt I was, I never let them know. I would just stick my nose in the air and walk on by, but inside, inside, I was on my knees begging to be accepted, to be liked. I had been told many times I was too dramatic. I tried to change, but it seemed the more I tried to be like somebody else, the more dramatic I got and the loneliness it gave me was excruciating. At least my family wanted me and needed me.

As soon as school was out I would go straight home and take care of Jimmy so Mother could shop and do other things. I raised Jimmy and later on Charles. That's why I have no desire to have children now. I've already had mine. My brothers.

The most thrilling moment of our lives came when we were told that our church was going to build us a house. They had the finest architects in North Carolina design it and, for once, we had something to say about what we wanted and how we wanted it. Watching the foundation, watching that beautiful house go up gave me a feeling of really belonging to something. That house was ours. Mother was deliriously happy because for the first time in her married life she could select the kind of furniture she liked, the color schemes she wanted and when she chose pink for the bedroom Daddy had a fit and said, "I'll never sleep in a pink bedroom! Over my dead body!" He did though and he liked it because a year after we moved into our new home, Charles was born.

The first day Mother threw up I was downstairs with little Jimmy and I heard her and thought, *Oh, no. Another baby to take care of.* It wasn't that I didn't love Jimmy or had ever been jealous of him. On the contrary, I adored him and tending to him was like being a mother, but even though I knew a lot of the kids didn't like me, there were some who did and I so wanted to have the freedom they had. I wanted to be popular and have loads of dates and go to the drugstore every afternoon after school like they did and sip Cokes and flirt. When you are very young, you don't always understand your responsibilities. I knew by then, believe me, that I was *the* minister's daughter and could not do all the things they did, but it certainly didn't stop me from wanting to. I was dying to smoke. I wanted to smoke, smooch and swear like they did but I knew I could not. I owed my daddy this respect. I couldn't say hell and I couldn't say damn, but damned if I didn't want to. I was very bewildered by my feelings because guilt was heavy on my heart. I was not supposed to think that way or to be like other kids because it could hurt Daddy's reputation. It wasn't that I didn't love my

parents, God knows I did, and proved it all of my life by sup-
pressing my desires and being good. How horrible it was always
to be good.

I was very active in the Methodist Youth Fellowship, naturally. It was the only way I could have any sort of social life. I
got to go on picnics and hikes which I loved and still do. At
least I got to be close to a lot of people my own age. Oh, I had
my share of boy friends I guess, but the ones I wanted were
wild and wild boys stayed clear of me.

I was always being held up by parents as an example, which
made the kids despise me all the more. "Why can't you be like
Little Margaret? She's so refined and so sweet." "Margaret Mc-
Larty doesn't smoke, why can't you be like her?" It was Margaret
McLarty this and Margaret McLarty that. So painful for me
and what could I say to them? Be glad you're not me? I wanted
to, but I could not. One girl at school, Gray, liked me and I
just thought she was wonderful. She was sporty and had a real
flare for handling people. We became great friends until one
day when she was at an M.Y.F. meeting and her sister said,
"Gray, you look terrible! Your elbows are dirty and your knees
are dirty! Now, look at Margaret. She is always dressed so nice
and clean. Why can't you look like Margaret?" That was the
end of our friendship.

The next summer, which was just before my sixteenth birthday, I went to Camp South Toe as I had the previous summers
after we moved to Marion. This is a religious camp and it is
named after the South Toe River which comes from the under-
ground streams of Mount Mitchell. The water is liquid ice, but
we used to swim in it and turn a beautiful shade of blue.

At camp, along with all the artsy-craftsy things, we were given
a weekly task. Our instructions were posted on the bulletin
board and, one week, I saw I was to clean lanterns. That's what
I thought it said because I couldn't spell too well back then.
Okay, I set to work. There were ten cabins and each one had a
couple of kerosene lamps hanging from the ceiling. What a nasty
job they had given me! I cleaned those things by way of stacking
two chairs one on top of the other and balancing myself to get
the lamps down from the ceiling, emptying out the kerosene,

washing them, refilling them with kerosene and then balancing myself to get them back up on the ceiling.

Kerosene is not the best thing in the world for lily-white hands and long, tapering nails. By the end of the week my hands were falling off and my nails were a memory. The camp gave awards for those who did the best job, and I won the Butt Award! They said they had never seen such dirty latrines in all the years of camp! Latrines? What were they talking about? Poor me. Yes, that had been my chore. Well, because of my mistake, it almost caused Daddy to lose his life.

That Sunday after my comeuppance Daddy, as usual, was to give the eleven o'clock worship service and he didn't show up. We waited and started singing hymns to pass the time and finally we ran out of hymns and started singing funeral hymns which did me in they were so morbid. And I was glad I hadn't been running off like the others all the time and smoking. Those hymns were getting to me. One was "There Is a Fountain Filled With Blood." It was at that point I was glad I hadn't committed the awful sin of bringing a dirty old cigarette to my lips because that leads to other sinful acts, you know. All this sadness was washing me away in my own tears and then, when we ran out of songs, we suddenly heard a faint horn off in the distance. We went outside to investigate.

We followed our ears and there stuck in a raging torrent was Daddy in a truck. You see, since I hadn't taken care of the latrines, they had asked my daddy if he would mind, since it was an emergency, to bring a truckload of toilet paper. The poor man had been blowing that horn all the time we were singing those hymns and, naturally, we couldn't hear above the sound of our celestial voices.

To get to camp you had to cross a shallow stretch of water and you had to drive real fast to get across, but we had had days of rain and that shallow part wasn't. Daddy had been afraid to leave the truck because he didn't want to lose it with all that toilet paper floating down the river, so we all pushed the truck across and saved the toilet paper and my daddy. He teased us about it. "This is a very undignified position for a preacher to be in."

That summer I really fell in love. It was at that time I discovered boys are not just something to get. His name was Eric. He was very sexy looking and we liked the same things. He shared my deep love of the mountains and we would take hikes and just sit and be quiet. He talked to me like a person. He told me about a girl he was in love with and the way he spoke of her astounded me because I had never known that boys could have deep feelings like a girl. I never forgot him and when we moved to Asheville, two years later, I saw him again. I also stopped seeing him again. He asked me out for a date and we stopped off "just for a minute" to see a girl he knew. She came out in a robe and said, "Eric, I want to show you my new bathing suit." That must have been some suit. Two hours later he came back in the living room, all fagged out. I knew what they had been doing while I played Solitaire. He wasn't as deep as I had thought. That was the end of my love for Eric.

But, after camp, when my birthday rolled around, I had a beautiful garden party. When I woke up that morning I felt very special. Everything in the day was special. I was sixteen. I was really grown-up. I didn't have to pretend anymore. It had finally happened.

Daddy's brother, Furman, who was at that time a professor of philosophy at Duke University, sent me a dozen long-stemmed red roses. He and his wife, Betty, knew how important that birthday was to me because only ladies got roses. Daddy ordered a Loretta Young movie for my party and he borrowed the movie projector and all the equipment from the church. Our garden was truly a work of art. Uncle Tokie's. He designed it and put up a fence with lovely climbing roses around it. Mother made me a beautiful hoop skirt formal and when each of my guests arrived, I stood at the entrance to the garden, where I had a table set up to receive my gifts. One boy said as he came up to me, "Is this the admission to the party?" and handed me a gift. I said, very seriously, "Yes, it is." Well, it was! Dear me was having her sixteenth birthday. Pay tribute!

Everybody was seated in the garden and Daddy showed the movie, then refreshments were served (Mother made and decorated the most beautiful cakes) and that was the party. I said,

"Let's sing 'Good Night, Ladies.'" We did and I then said good-bye.

After they left, Elizabeth Cross, my child friend, and I sat on the floor in the house and I opened all my presents. The reason I waited was that I was so afraid if I liked one gift more than another it would show in my face and I would hurt someone's feelings. In doing what I did, I probably hurt everybody's. I later got the word that they didn't like my idea of a birthday party. They said I acted like it was a stage play. Well? Wasn't that what life was all about? But it really was brought home to me when I was in a play called *Sunny of Sunnyside.*

I had tried out for the lead and I wanted that part of Sunny so bad I couldn't sleep nights. Eva, the girl who stuck up for me that time I fainted in class, beat me out of the part. Another blow. I thought she was my friend. . . . She really was and is. Today, she's one of my biggest fans and comes to see me in stock productions or Broadway shows. But, back then, it seemed she was anything but a friend because I felt that she should surrender the role to me since I wanted it a thousand times more than she did. She didn't. And one day during a rehearsal, some smart aleck said, "You're no different on stage than off. You're so dramatic you make us sick. What's the matter with you?" I was very puzzled. "I don't know. I'm an actress!" I could not understand why I should be different on a stage. To me, there was no separating the two.

The following summer, Daddy told us we were moving to West Asheville in September. We had lived four years in Marion and even though I had been an outcast much of the time, there were some kids, I believed, who would really miss me. Elizabeth was the dearest friend of all and leaving her was a painful experience. I dreaded that day when we would have to say our last good-bye.

The M.Y.F. gave a farewell party for me and I was so thrilled because I just knew they would be extra special nice and all the boys would dance with me. I really thought they would miss me. All the years I had lived there and been active in the M.Y.F., I had taught the kids a lot of folk dances so most everything they knew, I had shown them. Having moved around as my family had, I naturally picked up a lot of dances and that had been one of my duties—to teach them to dance. Okay, the dance began. I participated in all the square dances, naturally, and was having the time of my life, even though it was a sad occasion, but when the romantic music started and everybody paired off not one single boy asked me to dance. I was destroyed. I sat in the corner all night and played blackjack with poor Bill Suttle, who had a broken leg. If he hadn't had a broken leg, I bet he would have danced with me.

That last Sunday, Elizabeth came to say good-bye. She looked so beautiful and so sad. We didn't know what to say to each other so we just sat quietly and looked at each other. She had on a black velvet coat that fit at the waist and then flared out. The long sleeves were cuffed in white lace and at the collar. She looked so beautiful and finally she started to get in the waiting car and she suddenly hugged me and her long dark hair brushed against my tear-stained cheeks. She whispered, "Good-bye, little sister." Which was so precious yet so strange since I was much older. That was the last time I ever saw her. She was killed in an airplane accident a few years later and I knew it was going to happen at the instant the accident occurred. We wrote often, but we never met again. If there is a hereafter I hope we can be friends there.

4

Living in West Asheville meant being near Nanny and Uncle Tokie and other members of our family whom I dearly loved so it filled some of the emptiness at being parted from the few friends I once again had to leave behind. I was now a senior in high school and moving is always a problem for any young person, even if you are accustomed to it. It means proving yourself and trying to be accepted, which for me were always difficult because I was different. I was the untouchable—the minister's daughter.

I was a pretty girl, not beautiful, but pretty, so I was an immediate threat to all the girls and they wasted no time in staking their claims on boy friends. Whatever was left over, I was welcome to. Again, not having any close friends, or even close acquaintances, I became active in the drama group and in the glee club. This was my loneliest time of all because I was seventeen. I'd been grown-up for a whole year and I wanted lots of boy friends because marriage was out there just waiting for me. I don't know how I thought I would manage both careers but I didn't think about that. I wanted to be popular with the boys.

I finally got a boy friend. Jimmy. Back then, the fad was to keep your books in your boy friend's locker. So, one day I went to meet Jimmy between classes to pick up some books and he opened his locker with the meanest bang and threw my books on the floor and yelled, "Here are your books and stay away from me, you slut!" Jimmy was such a nice boy and I had never seen him angry. I knew the word slut was bad because of the way he said it, but I was not familiar with the terminology so I couldn't quite figure what he was mad about. He slammed his locker shut and stomped off.

I stood there bewildered by this and I noticed that all the kids were snubbing me as they passed by. Not one person would speak to me. All the boys were looking me over and I mean up and down and laughing at me. Finally, I grabbed Lewis, a boy who had once been nice to me. "Lewis, what is wrong? Why are people treating me like this? What have I done?" He jerked his arm away and looked me over, too. "We understand that you do it with everybody." "I do what?" "Well, I don't know if I should be caught talking to you . . ." and he started walking away. "I do what?" I grabbed him for dear life. "Look, you should know what you do and what you don't." He walked off and I just stood there feeling as though the end of the world had been announced.

Somebody, no doubt a girl, had started horrible gossip about me. It was so unfair because I didn't even pet in those days and it made me so mad because it was untrue. I had been proper all my life and held boys off magnificently as I had been taught to do for my daddy's sake and my mother's sake and my brothers' sake and the whole McLarty family's sake and I probably did have boys on my mind, but I was very proper and had never done anything to hurt my preacher daddy's reputation. I had never let myself go with anyone and I began to get furious that I was being condemned for something I hadn't had the pleasure of knowing or doing.

I went to the dean of women, Mrs. Hoffman. I had to get this horrible lie straightened out. I could just see my poor daddy being kicked out of his church because of his wayward daughter who had become a slut. By the time the gossip reached him I would probably also "be with child." Mrs. Hoffman didn't want to talk to me at first. It was quite clear that she knew all about it. I insisted she listen to me. This was *my* life everybody was enjoying wrecking. After I explained how I suspected it all started, and told her about myself, she was so sweet and felt sorry for me. She was very strict and all the girls hated her because of it, but from that moment on, I was her greatest fan. She said, "Margaret, the only thing you can do is simply go ahead and do your work. Do what you have to do and ignore them until it all dies down." She hugged me. "You'll see. It will be forgotten in no time." It was, but that day left quite a scar.

Happiness was suddenly mine. The greatest thrill of my life came when a good-looking college boy asked me to a DeMolay dance. Mother had a fit because he was older than I, but I was not going to pass up so wonderful an opportunity. Besides, other girls would faint from jealousy. I was so desperate to be popular, to belong to a crowd, and the DeMolay dance could be the golden key. I would look beautiful and all the boys would realize how desirable I was. Of course the fact that I had an awful cold and my nose was stopped up and red as a berry, didn't bother me. I would overcome. Mother relented when she saw how determined I was.

Once we got to the dance I hardly saw my date. Loads of boys danced with me despite the fact that I had the sniffles and had to keep a handkerchief handy every moment and my cold got worse until I could barely talk. I was in heaven. Then, as I was snubbing a girl while my date whirled me about the floor, I suddenly saw him passing money behind his back to a boy who had just danced with me. That was a very bad feeling because then I knew why so many boys had asked me to dance. He was paying them so he could be free to be with someone else. I died of shame. Obviously he had asked me out in order to get to the dance to see someone he was in love with.

It wasn't as disastrous as I thought because soon after, a boy I had had a crush on from a distance, Bill Troward, asked me for a date. He was a member of the DeMolay's, too. We went on picnics, lots of dances, movies, all the things a girl is supposed to be doing. Then, I started dating other boys, too. That snooty college boy had opened that hidden door for me after all.

I was very active in the drama group and that spring we went to Chapel Hill for the big festival, where the high school students all over North Carolina got together and auditioned for the summer theater there. My drama teacher was very excited about a play she wanted me to be in and I was just as eager to get the part, but Bill said, "If you go to Chapel Hill this summer I will never date you again." I wanted to be in that play, but Bill was my steady and I couldn't bear the idea of being in high school the rest of the year without a steady boy friend. Fool that I was, I gave up the chance and didn't go. But, fate was not going to lose me to Bill. An outdoor pageant, *Thunderland*, was being done in Asheville. Lamar Stringfield wrote the music and a cousin of mine was doing publicity for the show. She thought I should meet Mr. Stringfield because she knew how desperately I wanted to be an actress, so she took me to see the show and then she introduced me to him. My cousin's hunch was right. He became a great influence in my life and later, when I was in college, he wrote me that he wanted to manage me. He asked me to quit school and come to New York. He said he would make me famous. But, that day, he asked me to sing for him and I did. He was very pleased and wanted me to be in *Thunderland*, but that did not work out. He told me he had written a musical called *Carolina Charcoal* which was to be done that summer in Aberdeen, Virginia, which has the oldest stock theater in the country. He asked if I would like to audition for the part of Carrie. I read the script and I got the part.

He took the Equity members who had been in *Thunderland* to be in the musical. The day I read for the part, all these hotshot professionals from New York were stunned that this hick kid could act so well and, of course, the peacock in me came out in all its brilliant splendor, but later I turned into a sparrow because when rehearsals began, the Equity actors started directing me. The Carrie I portrayed was lost somewhere between all the varieties they shoved at me. They all had different ideas of how I should play the part so when they got through with me, the character was lost completely. Disaster.

During rehearsal for the show, I was taking voice lessons from Lamar Stringfield and paying for them by copying music and sometimes I would cook spaghetti for everybody. It was at that time I learned how to make it the way Italians do.

We rehearsed at his house where they kept apple cider in the kitchen which they would spike sometimes. The first time I tasted it I thought, *Oh, this must be the way hard cider tastes.* I didn't know it had been spiked and I loved it so I was in the kitchen nipping a lot that night. They knew what I was doing and thought it was pretty funny. When I discovered I couldn't walk they told me I was stoned and why. They filled me with lots of spaghetti and garlic and gave me a clove of garlic to chew on so my parents would not smell the liquor. They got me sobered up and took me home. I smelled so bad my family wouldn't come near me so I got out of what might have been a horrendous ending to a pleasant experience.

The night before we were to open in Aberdeen, Mr. Stringfield was driving up with his lady friend and he asked if I wanted to ride up with them instead of waiting until the next morning and going with the rest of the cast. I asked my parents and they said I could but when all the kids started making insinuations, "Oh, you're going up with Lamar, hunh?" I knew there would be gossip so I didn't go.

I bombed in the part. I felt like a fly caught in a spiderweb. I never should have listened to all those New York actors! And when my parents drove up to take me home, an old character actor who hadn't said much to me from the very beginning, rode back with us. We hadn't been in the car twenty minutes before he growled, "You were terrible in that part!" My mother got all upset and she said, "She was not! How dare you!" And he said, "Now, you just be quiet. Now, girl, listen to me. You've got talent and when you read that first day you were marvelous, but you know the problem with you is you listen to too many people. You should have played it exactly the way you read it that day. Your instinctive feeling for the character was right. If you really want to be an actress then you've got to go ahead and do what you think is right. Listen only to yourself and what your *self* tells you to do. When you're on that stage, girl, you'd better believe that all you've got is yourself." Mother couldn't stand him for blessing me out, but I bless him to this day because he was so right.

My mother had gone to Greensboro College so it was only fitting that I, too, should attend Greensboro. I considered majoring in home economics because by then I had been thoroughly brainwashed about being a woman and preparing for your future as a wife to some nice, respectable man.

My first day at college I walked into the home ec. lab and instantly knew it was not for me. I had studied voice and music all of my life so I dared to sing for the voice teacher, Mr. Williams. I knew that my parents hoped I would graduate, get a job close to them and eventually get married and raise a family. I wanted to get married, but I wanted to be an actress and a singer. I had never forgotten the time in New York when I was a little girl, standing on the empty stage at City Center and Mother had led me away as I said, "Someday, you'll see—I'm going to be a star."

They didn't think I would pursue a career in the theater when I got out of college. There it was ". . . face reality." I didn't want to hurt them so I didn't think beyond the moment. When I sang for Mr. Williams, he said, "By all means, you must major in voice." I took the music tests and got the highest grade possible. I double minored in music theory and drama and devoted very little time to the other subjects.

One day, during my freshman year, I was on my way to a class and Elizabeth crossed my mind. I had gotten a letter from her a few weeks back telling me her father, Semion Cross, had bought a plane and she couldn't wait to fly in it. And I panicked when I read those words. I remember thinking, *No, Elizabeth! Don't ever go up in that plane!* I guess I still had that feeling when she flashed in my mind and I thought, *I wish she were here.* And shaking the uneasiness I felt, decided to write her that day and invite her to visit me. I knew she would like Greensboro. That afternoon I received a call from Mother. The plane I had prayed she would never go up in had crashed in Black Mountain and there were no survivors. I couldn't stop crying. It was so horrible. Such a waste of a wonderful girl who had so much to live for and so much to offer. But, she was gone. And a big piece of me went with her.

When I got home Mother was crying, too. The shock I felt was only comparable to Mother's. She had loved Elizabeth and knew well how I cherished her friendship. Mother had also gotten a feeling that something had happened to them. She said she was in the yard hanging laundry and a hard, fierce wind suddenly came down and started banging and twisting the sheets and she said aloud, "Semion Cross! There's something wrong with Semion Cross!" She ran in the house shaking all over and at that very instant the phone rang. Daddy told her Semion's plane crashed in Black Mountain. He and Elizabeth were flying two boys who had been visiting in Marion back to Asheville and when Semion started to take off the men at the airport had advised him not to fly because it was too windy, but told them he could handle it.

Elizabeth was only fifteen when she died, but at least she got the one thing she wanted—the world championship. It's hard to talk about her—even today. Time does *not* always heal all things.

For the next few months, until I could live with my grief, I became active in everything I could find to do. I wanted to be busy every minute of every hour until I could accept the fact that she was gone. "Good-bye, little sister."

I was in every play I could get in and very active in the M.Y.F. During my sophomore and junior years I went to the summer conferences in Lake Junaluska. Beautiful country. The dormitories were set in lush woods so thick you found yourself listening at night for the sounds of lightfooted Indians. Up there, I was a different person. I was myself. I was really liked. People came from all over the world and it didn't matter that I was a preacher's daughter. They couldn't have cared less. I was elected the head of the Western North Carolina Youth Fellowship recreation program my sophomore year. And I was to go all over the state, which I did and loved and where I taught the various groups folk dances.

The next summer I was elected to represent the M.Y.F.'s Western North Carolina Conference at the Baltimore M.Y.F. Conference. I didn't know until I got there that it was an all-Negro group. There were five hundred Negroes from New York, New Jersey and Baltimore. And there I stood. Little white me. I was shocked at first only because no one had told me and I was scared out of my mind because it was at that gathering that I found out what it felt to be in the minority. The only blacks I had known were Susie, Reesie and my friend Audrey from Staten Island. But they went out of their way to make me feel welcome because they realized it was important to show me, a white girl from the South, that they are human. We forgot color and I had the most wonderful time of my life.

I adored my roommate. Every night we would group off and have the nightly prayer sessions. We would collect in someone's room, a bunch of girls, all in our nightgowns, and after prayers talk about the things of the day and, naturally, boy friends. One girl had on a baby doll nightie one evening and she was hugging a framed picture of her "true love." I thought, *We're all alike, God, why can't everybody realize this? What's the matter with people? Everybody loves, everybody has the same feelings.* I was very thankful that I had been given the opportunity to discover this.

When I left, we cried. All of us. Even some of the boys. I was only there a week but you would think I'd been there a year. I brought back five hundred pictures of my five hundred friends.

When I returned to the conference in North Carolina and began telling them of my wonderful experience with the blacks and how we must make every effort to rid ourselves of wrong thinking I was interrupted. No, I was stopped and dragged off the podium. It was the older counselors who were having a traditional fit, not the young people. If my daddy had been there he would have stopped them, believe me. "Go on, Old Girl, tell it!" That's what he would have said, but he wasn't there. I looked at those old maids and I thought, you poor bigoted fools. That was the last I ever saw of them or had anything to do with them. Later, the kids got me aside and asked me to tell them about it and I did, leaving nothing out, not a single instant. While I was in college, my family moved to Mooresville. It was flat and hot and very bigoted. I couldn't stand it there. That summer, after I had bid an unladylike good-bye to M.Y.F., I was getting ready to go to a revival service when Jimmy and Charles changed my plans (which I was very happy about).

Jimmy, like most young boys, decided to dig his way to China out in the backyard. He and Charles started working their way out of Mooresville and when they got down to about seven feet, they decided China was a bit far so Jimmy filled the pit with water thinking to have a swimming pool, but of course it was just another mud hole. He jumped in it, taking his cat with him, and Charles followed. Well, they came to the door hollering for me, as everybody else was filing into the church gasping at the two chocolate boys with the cat. Jimmy was holding it by the tail and its legs were sticking straight out along with the wet hair on its back, screeching in high C. The congregation continued to gasp and I was convulsed with laughter. I had to shoot them down with the hose and in the process got all wet, so by then it was too late for me to re-dress and go to the revival service. Pity! The three of us had a grand time reviving our souls in our own way.

This little display of "funfulness" was to the congregation a prize example of the lack of control my mother had over "those wild Indians." So, the church members filed their complaints. Their report reached Mother's sweet ears, which turned rather a stunning scarlet—with rage. They said Mother kept an "untidy house." And my brothers, like most children, had committed terrible crimes. They sometimes drew pictures on the walls of the parsonage. At other times, they were boys. Both acts were unforgivable. The minister's children were supposed to be perfect, "without sin." Earthbound angels. Mother was beside herself when she learned that the women had said she was a poor housekeeper. It isn't easy to pick up after growing boys every five minutes. Not when you don't have a maid and must do everything yourself. So she invited all the members to come over and inspect the house.

When I learned that these gossipy old women, these dried-up old maids were going to snoop through our home, Mother and Daddy thought they might have to lock me in the basement until it was all over. I was furious. Nobody had a right to see how we lived. And I was mad with Mother for being so hurt by their words. What difference did it make? I knew it made a lot of difference. A minister's life is an open book and that goes for his house as well.

Here they came. Men and women puffed up with their own absolute perfection, treading through the house, heads bobbing as they looked the place over. Well, their bobbing heads froze when they got to my room. There, covering the walls of my room were five hundred pictures of my five hundred black friends. Smelling salts were needed I am sure as soon as they floated out on their own huffing Christian breath. But Mother and Daddy showed that room with great pride.

My senior year, I won the best actress award for two different roles. For Prossy in *Candida* and Golux, an elf in Thurber's *Thirteen Clocks*. It was quite an honor and also most unusual because I did not major in dramatics.

When I learned we were going to do *Candida* I did everything I could think of to persuade our drama teacher, Dr. Mary B. Parker, to give me the lead. She told me I was not physically right for it. She saw me as Prossy. I had another of my first-rate tantrums. It did not help. Prossy or nothing. Okay, I made up my mind that I would really *make* this character. Prossy would dominate the stage. She did. It became one of the best roles I ever played. I got great reviews and my dad came to see me in it. He said, "Old Girl, you were really marvelous. I can't get over how good you were." That was the first real compliment I had gotten from him about my acting.

In the spring we did *Thirteen Clocks*. One day, during a children's performance, there was a sudden electrical storm and all the lights went out. The children began to scream, terrified by the storm. I don't know how I got the idea to do what I did, or what made me do it, but still in character as the elf I began talking to them, calming them, explaining that this was part of the show, that the evil spirits had turned the lights out. Soon I had them singing camp songs, they began laughing, having fun, and the terror passed.

Newspaper reporters came to see me, took pictures and wrote up a big story. All the papers covered it: of how I handled the children and averted panic. That was my first big splash of publicity. By accident. Every break I've ever gotten seems to have been by accident. I don't mean luck. That is something I do not believe in. We make our own, but I have accidentally done the right thing at the right moment or been in the right place at the right moment.

And meeting Norris Houghton will prove a point, because until that night, I had not faced myself honestly about my future.

Dr. Parker, my drama teacher (she looked like Judy Garland to me), was very enthusiastic about my acting ability and after *Thirteen Clocks* she felt I should meet Mr. Houghton, who was an authority on the great method teacher, Stanislavsky. He was giving a lecture on him in town. But I didn't know who the famous man was. I'd never heard of him—even though I was applying his system unconsciously. I thought it was funny that Dr. Parker would take me to hear a lecture on a composer. Well, you've got Stravinsky and so many other composers with names like that. But once Mr. Houghton began speaking about the great actor he had known so well, of course all was clear.

With every word he spoke, my passion mounted. I found myself thinking, *Yes, yes, that's the way it is. That's the only way to approach acting.* Suddenly I realized I had been clenching my palms and blood was running out of my hands.

The lecture ended and people clapped politely but no one was as savage as I to get to him. I shoved and kicked my way through the people and ran to him, my palms outstretched and bleeding. "Please, help me, I've *got* to be an actress!" My moment of reality had finally come. I didn't care anymore what my parents wanted for me. I knew this had to be my life! He was taken aback, as anyone would be to see this crazy-eyed girl, like some kind of nut, standing there, tears pouring down her cheeks and those bloody hands staring him in the face. He shook his head. "God help you." I said, "Yes, with or without His help I'm going to be an actress. Please. Help me." He took my face and said, "All right. You must study. You must go to the Neighborhood Playhouse in New York and study with Sandy Meisner. If you can't get acepted, get in touch with me and I will help you."

Years later when I was doing *Abe Lincoln in Illinois* on Broadway, who should be one of the producers but Mr. Houghton! The world is very small, you know. But as of that night, I knew what I had to do and nothing would stop me. I did not have the courage to tell my parents, but I felt the moment would come when it would be right. The moment came two weeks later. The glee club was to go to New York for a week to sing at Carl Fischer Hall. My dream had been handed to me with all expenses paid.

I immediately wrote a letter to Dr. Berger, the man who had been so understanding when I was living on Staten Island and who had arranged for me to go to P.S. 45. I told him I wanted to study at the Neighborhood Playhouse, gave him the date of our engagement at Carl Fischer and asked him to see me. I wanted him to help me get an interview at the Playhouse. He was now the superintendent of schools of Lower Manhattan and I felt his influence would get me in.

We went to New York by bus and sang every inch of the way. My heart was in my voice because I knew my life was now beginning. It was just a trip up for them, but for me it was the biggest step up I had made.

Victor Berger and his wife came to hear us and we spent some time together afterward. They were so kind and wonderful. I just knew that everything would work out because everything seemed so right. He made an appointment at the Playhouse for me and the next day Mrs. Berger took me to lunch and then to the Playhouse. We waited and waited, but no one would see me. From then on, I was on my own. I went back several times and on the third day I had an interview with Mrs. Rita Morganthau, the founder of the school. She was a tremendous personality. A tiny little dowager, jewels on every finger, and with eyes full of love—but she was tough. Tough in that she laid it on the line. She gave it to you straight and she didn't waste her words. She said, "Sandy Meisner will be the hardest man you could ever study with. You're a sweet, charming young lady from the South. This is rough work and it will often shock you. Mr. Meisner will try to tear you apart and he probably will. You won't last, but if you think you can try it, if you think it is worth it, then you are accepted." It was like being admitted by dear old Saint Pete.

I was to begin in September and the registrar asked me to send them a picture. I sent a snapshot. What did I know of glossy eight by tens?

When I returned home, I did not tell my parents what I had done. I did not feel the timing was right, but I hinted around, trying to see their reactions. A week later I went to Manteo, Roanoke Island, off North Carolina, to audition for the *Lost Colony* pageant. It was freezing cold that day and the wind was howling. They couldn't hear me over the wind and they kept saying so. Finally, "Thank you, dismissed." I could not accept that. What to do? I knew they were also auditioning singers for their choir, but I hadn't come prepared. I didn't have any music with me and I was freezing to death. So, I thought, eying the building where the vocal auditions were going on, at least I can get warm even if I can't get a job.

I marched over to the building and submitted my name. When my turn came I stamped up on the stage and said, "I didn't bring any music and I frankly don't care whether you hire me or not. My toes are frostbitten and I just came in here to warm up!" They thought that was pretty funny and asked if I would sing something I knew by heart without accompaniment. I sang a folksong and they liked it. They then asked if I happened to know Mozart's "Alleluja" and I said I did. "If you've got the music, I'll do it." I did, they loved it, and I got a job in the choir. Another accident.

That summer, packed and ready, I kissed my family adieu and hopped a bus for my first professional job. Sixteen hours later and very weary I arrived at Aunt Gracie's. Her claim to fame was playing the comic role every year. Aunt Gracie (as she was called by everyone) had a big house there and she would rent out rooms to the young people in the company. I was so exhausted when I got in that I went straight to bed. It was only 8:00 P.M., but I had had a rough ride and changed buses many times before I hit Manteo. The kids came in that night, anxious to get a look at the preacher's daughter, and when Aunt Gracie told them I was already in bed, they probably wondered what they would do with an angel-apple like me.

Aunt Gracie was quite a character. She was a grandmotherly type. On the plump side and she wore flat shoes. She had a shock of white hair with a pronounced widow's peak, and dark brown eyes that laughed all the time. She was gruff, but always funny. Well, the poor dear thought she would make me feel at home so before I went to sleep she asked if I would like to go to church the next morning. Well, I thought she always went so I said yes. That dear thing. She hadn't seen the inside of a church in years, but I didn't know that then.

I came down the stairs the next morning in a white dress and a white hat. As I descended the stairs I looked in the living room and there sat a baker's dozen—all staring at me. They were waiting to get a look at the preacher's daughter.

I showed them pretty-hot-spit-quick that I was a regular guy. I could shoot pool, better than some, so everybody sighed with relief and the worst was over that first week.

I was determined to get acting parts so I auditioned for everything that came along. They weren't what I wanted, but it was acting. I got all the mass scenes—you know, screaming, hysterical scenes. The company started calling me Little Sarah Bernhardt and they laughed at me because in every performance I would cry real tears. Then I got the lead in an opera as a Salem witch and did a tremendous job with it so the kids dropped the nickname. I was serious about my work and they finally realized it.

A number of boys from the show were staying at Aunt Gracie's and they became very protective of me. I dated a lot and they would wait up every night for me. They worried about me and that's the truth.

I had taken a part-time job working in a gift shop to make

extra money. I hoped it would make my parents less upset about my going to New York when they saw how much I had saved, which by the end of the summer was almost two hundred dollars. I thought I could live on that for my two years at the Playhouse!

There was a good-looking boy who came around to the shop almost every day to see me and, finally, I said I would go out with him. Now, I had casually mentioned to Ann, my roommate, that I was seeing him. After the show, he and I walked up on the sand dunes. I thought it would be very romantic and suddenly he grabbed me and pulled out a knife. "You know what I could do with this?" He pressed the blade against my throat. I don't know where I got my cool, but I calmly said, "Oh, just look at that moon." He repeated his threat and I said quite casually, "You could do a lot with it. Look over there. See that big cloud?" He was all undone at the way I was behaving. I was spoiling his fun, no doubt. He looked. "No, that's not a cloud, those are mosquitoes and they're heading for us!" They were. Millions and millions of mosquitoes swarmed down on us and I grabbed his hand. "Come on, we've got to get to the car before they eat us up!" I led him back to the car and he drove me home. When we got there I shot out of the car and said, "I don't like you. You're not very nice."

Now, the boys at the house nicknamed me Little Belle because I had so many dates, and when I came home that night they were all sitting there, smiling and relieved to see me. What I didn't know is that when they found out whom I had gone out with they had searched for me everywhere. Apparently that boy was sick and they knew about it. I don't know if they had anything to do with his disappearance or not, but no one saw him again after that.

When the show closed for the summer, a boy I had dated a lot back home drove down to get me. He brought Mother and several members of his family. They all stayed at a hotel and Mother stayed the night with me. My roommate had moved in with another girl so Mother could be with me. My meticulous cleanliness-is-next-to-godliness mother was appalled when she saw me, the room and the kids. I had just finished doing the witch thing and my hair was full of olive oil, ink and carbon paper to get it witchy-black and my pillow was as black as my hair. It was too hard to get the color to wash it out so I had gone to bed with my hair like that all week. Mother was really turned inside out. "How can you stand being so dirty? Look at this room. And all those dirty looking people downstairs. Oh, how disgraceful!" I was amazed because I had never noticed dirt or dirty people. Well, except for the john. We shared it with several boys and I must say my brothers never dribbled all over the floor like they did. That drove us girls crazy all summer. We had to use the cleansing powder before we could ever sit down. That was one toilet seat that Aunt Gracie had to give another coat of paint to after we left.

We were a couple of hours late getting home and when we pulled up to our house there was little Charles with a big placard that read, "Welcome Home, Sis." That cute thing with skinned knees and a mop of brown hair hiding sleepy eyes had been sitting on those steps for two hours waiting for us. Jimmy welcomed me in his own way. He gave me a frog.

When we got in the house I said, "I'm going to New York to study acting." I had harbored a dream all my life and now, just as on that night in City Center when I told Mother I was going to be a star, I had brought the moment of truth to the surface. It pronounced itself in the tone of my voice, the glow in my eyes and electrified my countenance. My parents stood there, helpless, because they knew this decision was not impulse. It had been the driving force behind all my actions and they surrendered me to myself that night for the first time in our life.

Mother's tears spilled into my heart like salt on an open wound, but I had to go. With every chosen bit of clothing that was carefully placed in my luggage, there were threads of recollections plucked at from every garment. I let Mother do the packing because I couldn't bear the tension of trying to select, or the nearness of her grief. I could think of nothing else except that I was about to create reality out of a thumb-worm dream.

With all the plays I had been in during college, and all the rave write-ups I had gotten in the papers, my parents simply thought it all very nice. To them acting had no substance like that of being a schoolteacher who got her salary every month. To act was to live in a bubble. They just didn't understand that some people cannot live rooted to a desk or a pulpit or in a rocking chair burping babies.

Mother stood in the doorway of our parsonage looking very little, waving good-bye with a river of tears flooding her cheeks. I had cut the cord and the pain was great for both of us, but I had to pursue my dream.

Daddy drove me to New York—New York, that gigantic electromagnetic force field that draws aspiring artists from all over the world into itself. The only thing I could think of was that soon my feet would be walking the pavements of that city I had fallen in love with the first time I had seen it. New York! The tires seemed to purr to the music in those two beautiful words as North Carolina grew more and more a memory with every mile. My two kid brothers sat eagle-eyed in the back seat looking at the scenery, not feeling my excitement and appearing a bit down in the dumps because I would no longer be around to be half sister, half mother. My imagination held me captive as scenes in kaleidoscopic pattern fashioned my future.

It was twilight when we approached New York City. My brothers sleepily rocked to the motion of the car, Daddy puffed on his pipe, looking to me every little while and I, in turn, would comfort him with an encouraging smile full of gratitude for all the years of love I felt for him.

As we sped along the highway I watched the city I was soon to be a part of change its color and its moods. This "ugly" city without form or symmetry, jammed up like the work of a pair of clumsy child hands—was mine! The cars, buses, trucks, raced along the weary asphalt that groaned under the billions of tons of engines and I thought, *Mine to know and be a part of.*

As we turned off on the exit that would take me to my new home, I smelled fall in the air. Even here, despite the smoke and spoil, fall was in the air. This ugly city was to me the most beautiful. And it would know my name before I left it! I wanted to jump out of the car and touch, touch, touch, everything I saw. From here on in I was free to live my dream.

Daddy had arranged my stay at the Alma Mathews Home for Immigrant Girls on Eleventh Street in the Village and he felt relieved that I would be under the protective care of nice ladies since it was sponsored by the Woman's Society of Christian Service. Daddy, Jimmy and little Charles were to stay at the YMCA for a few days until he felt I was properly ensconced and knew my way to the Playhouse.

We did the typical thing tourists do. We went sightseeing, spent hours in museums, the planetarium, all the usual, and saw a Broadway show. Naturally I sat through the entire production *being* the characters and knowing with such certainty that one day my family would come here to watch me in a show.

My first day at the Playhouse was spent signing in, finding out where my classes would be, and meeting teachers. When I met Martha Graham and Jane Dudley, well, that was more than I could take on a first day because I had read about these famous women in college and now to discover I was to be one of their students was faintsville.

I passed a girl in the hall who looked terribly familiar to me. We both turned around and started talking. We found out we had been passing each other for years. She was from North Carolina and had gone to U.N.C. in Chapel Hill. We had attended a lot of lectures and suddenly she said, "Now I know! You are the girl who ran screaming down to Norris Houghton with your hands bleeding." Well, who could forget a sight like that? Dasheila and I became good friends from that moment on. I knew Daddy would be pleased to hear there was another North Carolina girl with my notions. Dasheila had long, blonde hair down to her fanny. Her hair was the color of spun gold.

That afternoon while waiting for Daddy to pick me up, a man came out of the Playhouse wearing an outlandish orange shirt. I was being very condescending and asked if he worked there. I thought he was the janitor. He said, yes, he worked there and when Daddy drove up I nodded and said good-bye and hopped in the car. It was God. Sandy Meisner, but I didn't know it yet.

I had a lot of comforting things to tell Daddy. First of all, I had overheard the librarian say that she had to make a speech for the Woman's Society of Christian Service which surprised me, but I knew it would ease his worries about my being at the Playhouse.

Also, I told him in music class we sang a hymn, "Holy, Holy, Holy," so it wasn't Satan's Pit after all. Then I teased him that since he was a Methodist preacher and I was studying method acting that he need not worry—I would be just fine.

When they left I was sad to be parted from them, but thinking of all the fulfilling tomorrows drew away the veil of sadness between us. Jimmy and Charles stared into my eyes, each showing the big question: Why? Daddy looked wisely at me, pipe poised just so in the side of his mouth, puffing, studying me a moment. I could always read that kind and gentle face and I knew his silence was a prayer. Wishing me well, wishing me the fulfillment of my ambition. A new loneliness crept in at the corners of his loving brown eyes. Old Girl has grown up. She has her own world to find. A world beyond the mountains of North Carolina, a world alien to the McLarty clan.

As Daddy got in the car I saw him rub the back of his hand against his cheek. That all but destroyed me because I had never seen him cry before.

The first completely-on-my-own day I headed for the subway devouring every face, every building, keen-eared, listening to the noise of the city that sang for me, wanting to take the whole city into my arms, to skip with all my young and dancing heart, when suddenly I realized I was lost. I could not remember what train would take me to school. Oh, no problem I realized, everybody in New York has heard of my famous school. I only need to ask. I asked and asked. I began to panic now. God, I couldn't be late. Sandy Meisner might throw me out! "How do I get to the Neighborhood Playhouse?" "Where?" "Neighborhood Playhouse." "Well, where is it?" "On Fifty-fourth Street." "Where on Fifty-fourth Street? East or West?" "How do I know? Does it matter?" Finally, after getting on and off a lot of trains and spending all kinds of money, I saw a policeman. I was on the verge of tears. The policeman gave me directions and I wrote it down in big letters in my notebook so as never to go through being lost again.

I arrived on time by some stroke of good fortune or a slow-handed clock. Suddenly the whole class stood up and I heard, "God is coming." Well, when God walked in wearing that same orange shirt I nearly went to heaven with a sudden heart attack. I swear, I could actually see rays of light around him as he walked regally past his "chosen people." He nodded to the left and to the right and spying me he gave a pinched grin.

At some point in time, while he talked about the basic foundations of acting, he called me up to "do something." I was wearing my hair up, like a dancer's and had it teased over a bun. I'm sure they thought I had very long hair because when I asked what I should do he replied, "Oh, take your hair down and brush it." I yanked out the bun and they all laughed when they saw the length of my hair, which was barely to my shoulders, but I got out my brush and brushed. "Mar-ga-ret Mc-Lar-ty. Is that what people call you?" No, not quite like that, I thought, accustomed as I was to a Southern accent without hyphenation. "From now on, your name is Maggie." So, it was Sandy who gave me the name I hated, but I refused to spell it that way. I left off the "e." I guess with my soap-shiny face void of any make-up except lipstick, a skirt that was too long, I did look more a Maggie than a Margaret. I was still a knobby kid and stuffed my bra with stockings and hadn't acquired a "woman's grace."

Our work schedule was nine to five and several evenings a week were to be spent doing improvisations with a group. Aside from wanting to act, I also wanted to sing. I had studied with local teachers, some of them good, but to study with a New York coach who had possibly taught the greats was my burning desire. By the end of my first week I got up enough courage to speak to Sandy about the possibility of my taking a part-time job so I could take voice lessons. I knew no one was allowed to work while studying at the Playhouse, but I determined to plead my case anyway.

If I asked Daddy for the money, he would somehow find a way, but a minister seldom has much money and I did not want to be any more of a burden than I already was. I knew it wasn't easy for them so I kept my expenses down to the barest minimum. I didn't buy clothes or splurge on anything and lived on grits and potted meat sandwiches.

When I was growing up I had never been allowed to work like all the other kids. Through school it was always the same answer when I pleaded with my daddy to let me earn money for my clothes and school supplies. "Old Girl, if you really want to help us, you will stay at home. Mother needs you, the boys need you, and I need you." Once again at the Playhouse I was told I could not work.

After I explained to Sandy how I felt, how important it was to me to take voice lessons and pay for them myself, he reluctantly agreed, but if he saw that it was interfering with my progress he would insist I quit.

I got a job at Macy's selling hats. I worked Monday and Thursday evenings and all day Saturday. I worked under an escalator selling cheap hats. People would spit down from the escalators.

I sneaked in another job singing for the Union Theological Seminary on Sunday with a Wednesday night choir practice. On Tuesday and Friday nights I worked on improvisations with the kids if I didn't have to give a speech at the Woman's Society to pay for my rent at the Alma Mathews.

The nights I worked at Macy's I would take two potted meat sandwiches to class. One for lunch and one for dinner, which I ate while riding the subway to work. I found if I could squeeze my way through the rush-hour crowd, get to a pole on the train and wrap both arms around it, I could munch with one hand and sip a Coke with the other. But Wednesday night was treat night.

Just after I started singing at the Seminary I found a restaurant where some Columbia students ate. For ninety-nine cents I could get a whole meal. London broil, green beans, potato and dessert. For ten cents more I could have coffee. Also, they put out big baskets of fresh cinnamon rolls on all the tables, which I thought was very dear of the owners. I would wrap up a batch in a napkin and every Thursday morning would warm them and have them instead of grits.

I was on a tight schedule, but I had it worked out and there was seldom any conflict. As I said, I had to give a speech for the Society from time to time, but it never interfered with my jobs. Miss Hazel Hovell, our guardian angel at the Alma Mathews decided to take me off the podium and put me in the kitchen when she saw how much I enjoyed speaking before the ladies of the Society. And the trouble began.

Now, I had a cheerful, clean room and I loved the view. I could see the Empire State Building from my window and to me, that building was the symbol of New York. Looking at it restored my faith when I would think about my future and grow frightened. The rent was $7.50 a week, which did not include meals. Each girl had her own breadbox and her own section in the refrigerator. Miss Hovell was in charge of us and when I moved in, she told me that on occasion I would have to give a speech for the ladies. Miss Hovell was a very pious woman, proud and straight as a rod. The only way you could tell whether she was coming or going was by looking at her face.

The first time I was to give a speech we went to Paterson, New Jersey, for the great event. A number of girls who had addressed the ladies before were going so I listened to them in order to know what I was to say. "If it weren't for all you nice ladies, I'd be in the slums today." That sort of maudlin thing. I was so ashamed. Those girls were standing there stuffing the ladies with humble pie. I thought I would throw up. I was grateful to be staying there because it was safe and clean but I wasn't about to lose my self-respect as the price for appreciation. And those women were squirming. Nobody likes to be thanked by a beggar!

When my turn came, I told them how happy I was to be in New York, that I was here to study acting and that my daddy was a preacher. I talked of amusing things that had happened since I arrived. And went into an incident that occurred that morning when I was on my way to school. It was a lovely fall day and I decided to ride a bus and enjoy the sights. I asked a man where I could get a crosstown bus. He was Italian and with my Southern accent, he couldn't understand me. "I don'ta unnerstanda you," and he flailed his hand at me. I mimicked him. "Whata busa do I takea to crossa towna?" "Oh! The busa stopa righta here." They got a good laugh out of it and then I told them I also wanted to be a singer. Would I sing for them? Certainly. I did three songs. They loved it. Then I caught Miss Hovell's stare. That mouth was so pinched I thought she was going to swallow her lips. She gave me the sign to sit down. When we got home she said, "You were being a showoff." I wasn't. I was trying to give the ladies a treat instead of a treatment.

I became so popular that the Society would ask for me when

they had their meetings. I enjoyed doing it and I guess it just killed Miss Hovell. Christian duty means suffering and I was enjoying it. She put a stop to it and stuck me in the kitchen one Saturday to make pies. I was furious because a group of us from school were meeting that evening to do improvisations. She wouldn't let me go so I left all the pits in the cherries. It didn't take her long to realize pie-making was a dangerous risk where I was concerned so she had me helping with the cooking for a religious lonely hearts club, but again, I made it a pleasure and when she saw I was entertaining these lonely young newcomers she cracked the whip on that. Eventually she gave up on me and just let me stay on and considered it her Christian duty.

5

There were two young men in my class to whom I was attracted. They were both blond and blue-eyed, and one was named Bill. He too came from the South. Since almost every boy I'd ever dated back home was blond, blue-eyed and named Bill, I decided I liked him best. Our class had been invited to a Halloween party and I asked him if he would like to go with me. We went as Jack and Jill, but it wasn't until two years later that I broke his crown. I'm glad I didn't go with the other boy. He came to the party all wrapped in bandages as Jimmy Dean. Sick.

I didn't have much time for dating what with my two jobs and our improvisation groups, but gradually Bill and I saw more and more of each other.

About a week after my cherry-pit pies, eight or nine of us were to meet for a group session on West Eighty-fourth Street. Not knowing the city, I was unaware that certain neighborhoods were considered dangerous. At that time, this section had such a bad reputation that cabdrivers didn't even want to drive through there, but I was oblivious to the fact that I was in a crime-infested area.

I had forgotten the exact address so when I got out of the subway I started guessing. I had been there once before and I thought I would recognize the building, but the brownstones all looked alike. It was evening and the street was not bustling with the activity it knew through the day. Staggering shadows of bums appeared from time to time and, more than once, I had to step over dead-drunk bodies that had made their bed on the sidewalk or lay in a stupor on a stoop. Not knowing the address I was seeking, I started going in and out of all the buildings looking at the mailboxes. Young men would occasionally rush out a door and pause at the sight of me, but no one bothered me.

Not having any luck, I saw a store on a corner and I went in asking if they knew where Joyce lived—Joyce being the girl I was looking for. The store was Spanish, as was the neighborhood. When I asked where my friend lived, I got an answer in Spanish. They did not speak English and I was unfamiliar with their language. There was a phone booth in the store, but I didn't have a dime. I went outside, very upset now, and saw a policeman. I explained my predicament and he was kind enough to give me a dime. I called and told Joyce I was lost. When she asked me where I was, I was still lost. I didn't know the name of the store so Bill got on the phone and asked me to describe the store and he came and got me. When he told me how dangerous the neighborhood was I almost threw up. I guess people left me alone because I didn't know to be afraid of them.

That night, I was working on a scene with a boy named Charles. I took the character I was portraying quite seriously, and dramatically hit him. He hit me back. Reflex. Everybody was shocked. So was I. I snatched up my coat and flew out. Bill went with me. I'd never been hit by a boy before. I guess I deserved it, but I was acting out the part as I saw it, and so was he.

While Bill and I were on the way home, poor Charles called my house to apologize. He spoke to Miss Hovell and she told him I wasn't in. He said, "You tell Maggie I hope I didn't hurt her when I hit her." Miss Hovell hit the ceiling.

We had to be in by eleven so when Bill brought me to the door, Miss Hovell was waiting for me—without her teeth. She opened the door with, "Ith thith the young man who hit you?"

Bill and I laughed. She didn't. Bill left and she took me to her room, put her teeth in and gave me a lecture about the evils of the theater and how I was letting Daddy down because he was a minister and I should go back home and get married and have lots of babies. I was so tired that I leaned my head back in the chair and fell asleep right in the middle of her speech. I didn't mean to, but I had worked all day at school, put in four hours at Macy's and then had gone to West Eighty-fourth Street. She woke me up with a hard shake and snapped, "Go to bed and be glad you're sleeping alone!"

One Saturday night Bill met me at Macy's and we went to a diner for a hamburger. It was then I told him I had another job singing and I was working to pay for my voice lessons. Bill studied me for a moment, just like my daddy used to do, his forehead creased in worry lines and his eyes poured a look into me that made me feel all safe and warm. He took my hands and held them. "I really admire you. I wish I had your drive, but please don't make yourself sick. Will you promise you'll take good care of yourself?" He was so kind and I was genuinely touched by his concern. It was his kindness that led me to make the mistake of marrying him. And it was his concern for my well-being that led him to make the mistake of asking me. We were good friends and we should have kept our relationship on that basis, but when you are very young, love seems as important as life, for when you are young, to love is to live. To love someone and to be loved by them is always important, but our marriage was impulse. There's a big difference.

I had been at the Playhouse about two months when a lady in the office told me she had made an appointment for me with *Life* magazine for an interview. They were doing an article on young women who were the most likely to succeed in their chosen career. I had a week to get ready for this important event. I was positive they would select me out of all the actresses as the one who would make it to the top. I wrote my parents and washed out my black sweater since my sweater and black skirt were, I thought, the most appropriate to wear. I had a little white collar and white cuffs to go with it. This was my idea of the young girl who was going to make it. They would see this young thing looking so demure and just know without a doubt that when I put on a red sequin dress I could be the sexiest girl in the world. I knew it and I thought they would. They didn't.

The day of the interview arrived and there I sat in the office, looking down at Rockefeller Plaza, being very sure of myself and there sat a man listening to the story of my life and looking very bored. I was Miss Enthusiasm. The answer to his problem in finding *the* actress. I felt like I was saving him a lot of work. Here I am. You need look no further. Now you can concentrate on finding your lady doctor and lawyer and executive—I put on a big act and it ended in great disappointment. He finally said, "Uhh, what did you say your name is?" I told him. "Thank you for coming up." I walked out of there with my heart in my feet. I guess he looked at me and thought, *She's just a kid and she'll get married and have babies.*

Christmas time came around and I went home to be with my family for the holidays. They were now living in Kings Mountain. They were very happy to see me as I was to see them, but for every instant of joy there was an hour of sadness because it was taking me nearer to departure.

Earl, the boy I had dated a lot before I went to New York, came to see me and one night, right after Christmas, I made pizza pies for dinner. Since he couldn't drink beer in the presence of my family, I mixed ginger ale in apple juice to give it a little zing. After dinner, my parents left us and I built a fire in the fireplace. It was very romantic and I was going to tell him I was in love with Bill, but they looked so much alike, it was as though I were with Bill. He mentioned something about marriage and I didn't say anything. I just couldn't get up the courage to tell him about Bill. I already had Earl's class ring, his identification bracelet and his fraternity pin so we were kind of engaged, but it wasn't the same as really being engaged. I thought he would forget me when I went away and find another girl. I wasn't that serious about Bill, but I felt marrying him was inevitable. We were together constantly, we both wanted the same thing: it was only logical we would probably marry.

The next day I got a letter from Bill. He said, "I like you a hell of a lot. In fact, I love you." I showed it to Mother because

I thought it was so wonderful that he liked me, too. Then, I told her I might not come home that summer, but Bill and I might go back to Manteo and do the *Lost Colony* pageant. She said, "Then I suggest you get married first."

Soon after I returned to New York I began to get sick. I was not getting enough rest, certainly not eating properly and trying so hard to master my craft because the first year at school is a trial period. You don't know if you are going to be accepted back for your second year until after school is out.

The spring productions were soon to begin and as a first year student you don't perform. You work backstage. I got stuck with the needle, and sewing was not one of my talents, but that's what I had been assigned, making costumes, so I worked very hard on them. I was still holding down my job at Macy's but had to give up the singing job because of our schedule.

Bill and I were going steady now and he was getting worried about my health. (I have always been frail, but at that time I was as thin as a pin.) He lived near the school and he insisted I have dinner at his place on Wednesday nights since I was no longer getting my one wholesome meal at the restaurant near Columbia. Bill proved to be a very good cook and we had plenty of time to relax and enjoy dinner as we didn't have to get back to the Playhouse until seven. We had two hours. A luxury for me.

He really went out of his way to take care of me. He picked me up after work and saw to it I got home safely. He was so thoughtful and concerned about me that when he asked me to marry him I said yes. We became engaged in March. I did not want to get married. I just wanted to be an actress, but since we both wanted to act, I thought that would always come first, somehow, and I did think I loved him. I've since learned you can love a lot of people, but it doesn't mean you should marry them.

Our first fight was triggered a few days after he had given me a ring, over something that made no sense to me. We were having coffee in a diner one night and I said dreamily, "Oh, how wonderful the wedding will be. We'll have the biggest wedding in the world and Grandfather McLarty, Daddy, Uncle Emmett, who is also a preacher, will all conduct a grand and elaborate wedding ceremony." I clapped my hands in great excitement. "Now, Bill, we have to decide what kind of silver we want and what kind of crystal and china . . . " Bill turned purple with fury and yelled, "What is all this junk? China, silver! I just want you to be my wife. I don't want all that stuff!" "But Bill, when you get married everybody gives it to you. All we have to do is tell them what we like . . . " He jumped up and ran out. I paid the bill and every face in the place was on me as I chased out after him. He had an umbrella in his hand (he always carried an umbrella), and when I tried to talk to him he started beating it against the wall and yelling at me. I was terrified. I had never seen anyone lose control like that. I tried to explain that I wasn't asking him to buy anything, but not coming from a preacher's family and not being a churchgoer, he didn't know that when you get married people give you gifts. I stood there, frightened, wondering what had happened to the sweet, kind, gentle Bill I thought I knew so well.

That fight should have told us something, but it was forgotten and we set the wedding date for July. The truth was obvious, but we didn't see it. We were sorry we had committed ourselves and neither one had the courage to say it aloud.

When school was out my mother came up to help me pack and to meet Bill. She adored him and Mother made the observation that he was a lot like Daddy. Not so much in looks, because Daddy has dark hair and brown eyes, but the way Bill took over and managed everything. He was wonderful to her and I was very proud of him. When he said good-bye to me at the train, I should have been bursting with happiness knowing that we would be married soon, but I wasn't. Mother was so thrilled and I was so afraid we were making a mistake.

I got sick on the train and started swelling up. By the time we got home, the pain was excruciating. I had good reason for being sick. I knew that Earl would be there and that he half expected me to marry him and I didn't know how to tell him. So, I did a shameful thing. I sent Mother over to his house to tell him and to give back his class ring and all.

The day I arrived home, Mother sent for a doctor. He couldn't determine what was wrong with me so I suggested maybe mononucleosis? He thought that just might be it, but the blood tests showed nothing and I continued to get worse. I guess I was so scared I was ill from it.

Bill knew I was sick and he came to visit me. Daddy liked him instantly, which pleased me and relieved some of my fears. I just had a good case of bride's nerves, I told myself. Every girl in the world probably goes through a fright like that.

When Bill left, he sent flowers every day. He loved me. I loved him. There was nothing to worry about.

One day I dragged myself together and went with Mother to pick out the china. We were in the store, browsing, and all of a sudden I felt faint. I fell against the counter and Mother grabbed me, motioning to the saleswoman to help her. They took me in the back of the store and sat me in a chair. The woman stuck smelling salts under my nose and gave me a look I remembered well. It was like the time in high school when Jimmy called me a slut and I wanted to slug her. It was like, *Hmmm, she's pregnant and she has to get married.* I wanted to say, "You idiot, I'm sick—not pregnant!" And she probably calls herself a good Christian woman. I couldn't wait to go back to that store in the tightest dress I could find and show off my flat tummy—which I did a couple of months later. Some people have the meanest minds.

When we came home, I went straight to bed. I didn't feel well to begin with, but that woman really upset me. I had just gotten under the covers when Mother called up to me to pick up the phone. It was Bill. "Hi! I'm in town and I'm going to work here until the wedding." I slid down between the twin beds, crying and thinking, *Oh, no, no, now I'm really caught. Nobody can save me now.* I said, "I'm so glad, Bill." And hoped he wouldn't detect what I was feeling because he was good and kind and wonderful. I convinced myself once again that our marriage was meant to be. Our marriage would be a great success like Newman and Woodward. We would become famous as a team.

Our wedding day had finally marked itself on the calendar. The gown Mother bought me was beautiful. I kept telling myself over and over that this was the happiest day of my life. *Smile, you're a bride. You are about to become one with your love.* All I seemed to become was more frightened. I felt like I was going to my own funeral. And now I know that Bill was feeling the same way. We did not want the responsibility of a marriage.

I remember standing in the back and focusing on Bill as I started down the aisle while all eyes were on me and giving him my most radiant bride's smile and suddenly getting to the altar and realizing I was smiling at the wrong boy! It was a boy I didn't even know. Bill didn't have a best man so one of the ladies from the church supplied us with her son who was home for the summer. Well, I was given away by Daddy. When Bill kissed me, that wonderful safe feeling came back and I thought, *Oh, God, I'll be perfect for you in every way.* He looked so handsome and his face just glowed like a little boy who had just recited the Declaration of Independence.

During the reception a lawyer friend of Daddy's came up to me and said, "This is one wedding knot that will never come untied." At that moment I felt like my wedding ring was around my neck.

The first night of our wedding trip (can't stand the word honeymoon; has a yuk sound to it) we stayed at the Grove Park Inn. My Uncle Furman had stayed there once and had told me what a romantic and beautiful place it was. Later, when he was told he had cancer and only had six months to live, that was one of the places he and Betty, his wife, went back to.

I loved Uncle Furman very much. He was Daddy's brother, and very handsome. He had black hair and black eyes and a black mustache. We were living in Asheville when the doctors told him he was going to die. I will never forget the day he came to tell us good-bye. He and Betty were going to spend his last six months doing all the enjoyable things they hadn't had time for. I had to stay in my room because I had a terrible cold and we didn't want him to catch it so I waved good-bye to him from my window as they got in the car. What a horrible feeling that was—

Grove Park Inn was very romantic and very beautiful, just as Uncle Furman had said, but they didn't have air conditioning. The next morning we had breakfast in our room. We were on the American Plan, which I'd never heard of, but I was told I could order anything on the menu so I ordered *everything* on the menu. I was starved. I had cantaloupe, orange juice, cereal, an omelette with bacon, sweet rolls and coffee. What an appetite for a bride. The cook spread the word because poor Bill couldn't eat and they didn't leave that part out.

That day we drove to Florida and I burned up on the beach. The next morning I got up very early, ready to make a dash for the ocean, but poor Bill was exhausted so I left him asleep. I had more *energy* for a bride. The horrible sunburn wore me out more than anything.

We returned to New York and stayed in a hotel temporarily while Bill looked for an apartment. I remember one day, he came in all worn out and he said, "All you have to do is lie here and keep cool, calm and lovely while I trudge all over town, walking my feet off for you to get you an apartment!" We were not in a perpetual state of bliss.

One afternoon, when he came in dragging himself, I had figured out how to best spend the twelve dollars we had gotten from somebody, for house gifts. So I said, very proud of myself, "We do not have a toaster and we do not have a coffee pot so with this money I will be able to buy both." He lost his temper. "That money is going to be put on rent for the apartment."

I said, "We can't. That money was given to us to buy a gift. I have to write them and say thanks for the money, I bought a coffee pot and a toaster. I can't write them and say, thanks for the money. I got an apartment with it. It's only twelve dollars. What kind of an apartment can you rent for that?" We had a stinking fight. It was the kind of fight we had had over the china and stuff in the diner. I couldn't reason with him and he ran around screaming and banging furniture and I ran to the window and threw it open because I wanted out. It was fifteen stories up. I really didn't want to live because I could see that our marriage would be one round of arguments and fights. Just as I was about to jump, Bill caught me and we kissed and made up.

A couple of days later we moved into a one-room apartment on Ninety-sixth Street and Central Park West. It was small, in a nice brownstone, and it had potential. We took it because it had a large storage closet and we had to have space for storing all the wedding presents that were never opened until a few days before our divorce.

We both had our letters of acceptance back at the Playhouse so there wasn't much time for getting settled before classes started again. We had very little money so we kind of fixed as we went along. We got the most important things—a bed and a table with two ice-cream parlor chairs.

The day after we moved in, we were sitting at our little table having lunch and I said, sighing, "Just think. A week from today we will start back at the Playhouse." He said, "It's a week from tomorrow." I said, "No, a week from today." He got so mad he took the table and jammed it into my stomach and my sandwich almost came up. "You think you know everything. You always have to be right!" I *was* right, which made him all the madder and we screamed and yelled and threw things at each other. Then the doorbell rang, which ended the fight. It was the lady next door asking if we had any matches. What I think she was trying to do was put out the fire. All of our fights, and there were many, were childish, but then, we were children. A lot of young people are very mature at twenty-one: we weren't.

We managed to get the apartment painted without throwing buckets and bought a few more things to add to our creature comforts. It didn't matter that we weren't living in grand style. The most important thing was the Playhouse. I remember once, a couple of months after we had started back to school, we were late with the rent and the landlord came to our door. "Oh, my God, don't let him in." Bill was beside himself. He could just envision the two of us being tossed out in the snow with our bed and table and chairs and chest of drawers and all those unopened wedding presents. I let the man in and we had a lovely chat. He never asked us for the rent and I'm sure he was going to, but I guess he realized we were going to pay so he just visited and left.

That year was a rough one for us. We lived on faith. I could stretch a dollar better than the best. My weekly grocery bill could never exceed ten dollars. A can of beer was a luxury. We didn't mind that we had to watch every penny because we believed in tomorrow. We knew once we were graduated, the world would be ours.

One morning a lady in the office at the Playhouse called me in to tell me she had submitted my name to audition for a soap opera at CBS. I think the show was *Brighter Day*. They were looking for a girl to play a preacher's daughter; well, who could play it better than a real preacher's daughter? I was ecstatic. I knew without a doubt I would get the part. I went to CBS, very sure of myself, and was interviewed by the casting director.

She asked if I had ever done any television and I told her I had, but not in New York. I was too inexperienced to know then that sometimes you have to lie your way in, so I told the truth. The truth lost me the part. She wouldn't even let me see a script. It was so unfair. "Won't you let me meet the director and let him decide?" "No, it would ruin my career to introduce them to someone inexperienced in TV." I told her I had done a lot of TV in Greensboro, but Greensboro was like "Wormsville" or worse. Smalltown stuff! She was not impressed. "You might trip over the cables and embarrass us." Horrible woman! Well, I've been in television for nine years now and I still trip over cables, as does everybody else, but obviously the woman didn't know the cables aren't on the set with you. *Brighter Day* is off the air now—probably because they didn't hire me!

That experience got me mad. I decided I wasn't through with CBS. I had been carrying a letter of introduction from the producer of *Lost Colony* for a year and now that I had some of my grandfather's thunder and lightning, I decided to write to Robert Dale Martin, casting director at CBS, who was a friend of the producer. I wrote asking for an interview. No response. I called. He did not return my call. I wrote another letter and one night the phone rang. "Hello, Margaret?" I said, "Hey there, you crazy ol' thing. Where are you?" I thought it was Daddy. He said, "I'm sitting here in my office." There was a pause and he said, "This is Margaret, isn't it?" "Yes, isn't this Daddy?" He laughed, "No, this is Robert Dale Martin." I fainted. As I picked myself up off the floor, apologizing and stuttering, he said he called to make an appointment with me because his curiosity had been aroused by my letter since he had never heard of the producer of the *Lost Colony* who called himself a friend. He wanted to see the letter. That made me feel even more like a fool, but here was my chance. He would take one look at me and know I was right for something at CBS. He didn't.

A friend of mine at school prepared me for the meeting. I was to impress upon him that I needed a job desperately. Cry "poor mouth." So, I memorized my lines and went to meet Mr. Martin. "I want to work. I've got to have a chance. I'll push a broom across the set. I'll do anything, just give me a job." He leaned back in his chair, an unfriendly expression on his face. "You would push a broom? How about holding up a piece of scenery?" "Yes, yes, I'll do anything." He threw down a pencil he had been toying with. "This doesn't work with me, kid. That's an old actor's trick." I became cunning! "Oh, I was told to say this and I was just trying it out on you." My foxy line didn't help. He just sat there and stared at me. I got mad. "No, I don't want to push a stupid broom or hold a piece of scenery! I'm an actress and a good one, but be sure if I did shove a broom I'd steal the scene!"

He had me all figured out—he thought. He told me I was so sweet and obviously happily married and I should move back to North Carolina and be a good wife. His fatherly attitude choked me. "I've seen this so many times, my dear. Young girls just like you come to the big city, full of enthusiasm and give up. You'll never make it. It takes someone tough." My eyes were full of tears but I swallowed and gritted my teeth. I couldn't speak because I knew I would cry if I did so I just got up and walked out. Several years later he wrote a play and I auditioned for it. I read well and he got up out of that theater seat and walked down the aisle to me and said, "I have an apology to make. You've got what it takes and you are going to make it. I am seldom wrong about talent, but you are one young lady I was wrong about." I didn't get the part, but it wasn't because I didn't have the ability. I just wasn't the right type. I walked out of that theater feeling ten feet tall. That's probably the only time in my life I didn't mind losing what I wanted, because his words gave me all I needed to ever hear again. I would make it. My moment would come. Robert Dale Martin had confirmed what I already believed.

Our last year at the Playhouse was drawing to an end, which meant the beginning for all of us. I got the lead in the final play which is considered quite an honor. I wrote letters and sent pictures to a lot of agents inviting them to come to the performance so they could see me work in the hope I would get an agent. They came. It didn't do me any good because I wore Oriental make-up as I was playing the scullery maid in *Emperor's Nightingale* and they couldn't see what I really looked like.

Bill and I had an elevator mariage. We kissed and made up every other day. He would not let me work during our last year at school because he wanted me to concentrate on my studies. He wanted to give me every chance at my profession so he took care of our expenses. He was truly enthusiastic where my acting was concerned. He understood how important it was to me and this was one of the things I loved about him.

The night of our farewell party at the Playhouse was a stormy one. We went to somebody's apartment for the party and we were having a great time. All the "stars of tomorrow" were collected there. We danced, we had fun, it was wonderful and Bill came over to me with, "Honey, do you want to go home?" Well, I thought he was ready to go and so I said yes. We left and when we got home he said, "I'm going back to the party." "But, I thought you wanted to leave. Why did you ask me if I wanted to go home?" "Because you never let me have any fun so now I'm going back." I didn't say anymore because I was so hurt. I couldn't understand him. I wasn't jealous and he knew that. I was completely bewildered by his words. Today I understand. I didn't then. He wanted out and I did, too, but he faced it and I would not.

That night I couldn't sleep and I lay there listening to the sounds of the cars passing by. Every time I would hear a car stop in front of the building I would think, *There's Bill now,* sit up and put on the light, waiting, but he didn't come home until the next morning around eight. I got so mad because I was being left out. He was having fun and I wasn't with him to enjoy it, too. When he came home, I said nothing. I knew that this is what a good wife is supposed to do and I could certainly tell from the way he acted that just one word out of my mouth would begin the Fourth of July early.

He got a job as a waiter a few days later to keep us going. He worked hard and his hours were terrible and no matter how I insisted on going back to a sales job he would not consent. "You're supposed to be an actress. I'll make the money and you get a job as an actress. You're too talented to work in a damn store."

We didn't see much of each other when he started working because I started pounding the pavements in the early morning trying to get modeling jobs, auditioning for plays, and seeing agents while he slept. His job started at five in the evening which was about the time I usually dragged me and my portfolio in the door. He worked until 3.00 A.M. so the only time we saw each other was in bed. I didn't want to let days go by like that so I would set my clock and wake up before he came home. I felt it only right that we should spend a little time together, but my being awake seemed to make him angry. One night when I was waiting for him he yelled, "If I'm going to work myself to death for you then you'd better get up early and make rounds and you can't do it if you don't get enough rest!" I think he felt like Mother was waiting up for him. So all I saw of Bill was a zonked-out glob of protoplasm curled up in our bed as I climbed out each morning.

One morning while my husband was sleeping I got a phone call from a boy I had dated a long time ago back in North Carolina. He was in town for a couple of days and asked if I would meet him for lunch. I eagerly said I would and began rushing to get ready. Now, we had trouble with roaches. It was an old building and Black Flag was a household word, ever ready to halt the "March of Aïda." As I was sitting in front of the mirror I spied this two-inch-long roach waddling across the windowsill. I grabbed the can of killer and gave that ugly thing a good shower. Deader'n a door nail! Then, in my hurry, I accidentally used the stuff on my hair. Well, it was too late to do anything about it. I couldn't wash my hair and set it. So, I hoped the fresh air would blow away the smell, dabbed on cologne and away I went.

We met at the appointed time and as we hugged he took a deep sniff of me. "Oh, Margaret, I'm in love all over again. You smell just like I remember you. What are you wearing?" "*Black Flag.*" What did he know? He thought it was something exotic.

A couple of days after my romantic luncheon I got a job modeling preteen sizes in the garment district but they fired me the next day because they thought I was too busty for a preteen and I was so flattered I think I grew an inch.

I started getting modeling assignments for those confession magazines. *True Story*, things like that. I made it quite clear that I wouldn't do any obscene stuff. "No bra and panty scenes, no nightgowns. Nothing less than a slip." One scene I did was standing behind bars and crying. They gave me a bottle of glycerine and I said, "No thank you, I cry my own tears." Then, for the second half of that same story we went over to Brooklyn to shoot and I was to hang down from a cliff, having been thrown there by a car wreck. I was hanging there and supposed to look terrified of course and, at that moment, a huge rat ran out from under me. I didn't have to act to get the look they wanted.

After the shots were taken, the men were treating me to dinner. My clothes were all torn from the scene we had done and we pulled into a gas station so I could change. As I started toward the ladies room, the attendant saw me and ran over to me. He probably thought those men were gangsters and they were kidnapping me. "Hey, kid, what happened? You in trouble?" I didn't realize what he was thinking at that moment. "Oh, no, we were just taking pictures." He gave me that look I had seen twice in my life and suddenly saw me with different eyes. "Oh, I'll bet you were just taking pictures. They must have had fun doing it."

My confidence was at a high peak after getting that confession assignment. One hundred dollars was the most money I had ever earned for a few hours' work. And that morning as I deposited the money, I walked out of the bank just knowing that everything wonderful was coming my way. And coming my way on Fifty-seventh Street as I strolled along, looking into every face I passed, thinking that they would all recognize me very soon as Miss Famous, my portfolio clutched in my hand, was a man who suddenly gripped my elbow.

"You are just the right size!" Startled, I jerked my arm back and saw this bug-eyed little man, literally panting. "For what?" I demanded. "Oh, I beg your pardon. Aren't you a model?" "Yes." He pulled a card out of his coat pocket. "Look at my card." He passed the card quickly before my eyes and instantly returned it to his pocket. I didn't have time to read it, which was the idea, but I didn't catch on.

Very graciously now he introduced himself and told me he was an agent and I just stood there dumbfounded and said, "Unh, hunh." Country was written all over my face I am sure. He almost had himself a winner. *He* thought.

"I have a model just your size who was working for me and a big job came up today, but she didn't feel well. I think she had her period and uhh, the job really pays a lot. Fifty dollars an hour and there's four or five hours' work lined up and uh, you are a model, aren't you?" "Yes, I'm a model," and I held up my portfolio case. "You would be just perfect for the job. You don't mind posing in a bathing suit, do you?" This was the moment I had just known would come. And I thought, *I'm going to be a big star today!* "No, I don't mind posing in a bathing suit," and he already had me turned around and was walking me down the street as he kept up this fast patter and, "Well, as you have gathered I have worked with a lot of the greats," and he rattled off a lot of well-known names telling me it was he who had gotten them started in the business. "Where are we going?" I managed to ask, all aflutter. "Famous man, very famous man. Tycoon in the motion-picture world. If he likes you, you will be made today." He wasn't kidding.

We entered a fashionable building off Fifth Avenue and star dust wasn't only in my eyes, it was in my ears because if I hadn't been so square and so innocent I would have questioned the whole setup. All I could think of was, *Lana Turner made it sipping a soda! This is it! A star is born today!*

As we were going up in the elevator he said, "Now, if he should try to make a pass at you, you just be the perfect little lady you are and say, 'I don't go in for that,' and everything will be all right. Okay, sweetheart?" and he kissed me on the cheek.

This very distinguished looking man opened the apartment door and I felt like my heart would quit on me any second. The apartment was magnificent. High ceiling and big wooden panels, huge sofas, everything done in exquisite taste. Oh, I was so excited. The man asked me to sit down. I sat down. "Would you like a cigarette?" He extended a case of pink cigarettes toward me. Well, with my pink-and-green shirtwaist dress, I guessed he thought a pink cigarette would go nicely. "No, thank you." I only smoked with Bill. "Pink champagne?" And he reached for the bottle. "No, thank you." "Well, would you like to hear a funny joke?" I nodded and he told it. It was funny and I laughed. Then he told another that was a little shady. I sort of smiled. Then he told one that was really dirty. I got mad and he said, feeling confident—I guess he mistook my mad look for a sexy look—"Now, how about that champagne?" "No, but may I use your bathroom?" I was nervous. I always have to go when I'm nervous. He directed me to the bathroom, which was near the kitchen and they went in the kitchen and I heard him say, "How dare you bring that child up here? She's a baby. Are you trying to get us in trouble?" And the "agent" mumbled something and the man said, "You get her out of here. She doesn't deserve to be around a creep like you!"

We left in a hurry and the man had disappeared. This big-time agent wasn't through with me. When we got outside he started all over again, same enthusiasm. "Well, we still have another assignment. Guess you just weren't the right type for that guy." I knew things weren't quite right with this little man, but I didn't know how to get away from him. I was scared and he had a tight grip on my elbow. He marched me into a hotel on Central Park South and asked for someone but that someone wasn't in and, boy, was I glad. "You meet me tomorrow here in the lobby at two o'clock. This is a very important man. He pays a hundred bucks an hour and all you have to do is go out to dinner with him. If he likes you, he will put you in a Broadway show." And I thought, *I don't like this at all. What will Bill say?* Just to get away from the man I agreed to meet him the next day.

I rushed home and started babbling as I came in the door. Bill hadn't had his breakfast yet so maybe that's why he was so grumpy, but he yelled, "You crazy fool, if you've got an appointment just to have dinner with a man who might make you a star, you keep it!" I was hurt and amazed at my husband. I thought he would be angry and say, "I'll bust his head in!" But he went on, "Don't you turn down an opportunity like this. This might be your chance."

He said I should go so the next day I left to keep the appointment but I was walking very slowly because I was scared and it just didn't seem right to get paid so much money for having dinner with a strange man or any man. I didn't know what to do so I poked along hoping I would be a minute too late and the little man would be gone. A friend of mine from the Playhouse suddenly yelled at me from across the street. He was a real swinger and I thought he knew everything about everything. He came over to me and we started talking and I told him about the agent. "For God's sake, Maggie, have you lost your mind? I know who this jerk is and he isn't an agent. I also know who the man is you're going to meet. He takes dirty movies. My girl friend got picked up the same way you did a couple of weeks ago. And that rich man grabbed her clothes off." I started crying. "What am I going to do?" "Baby, come on, we're going for a Coke. Your two o'clock appointment is with me." We went in a drugstore and he told me a lot more about that agent. He was a pimp.

Two weeks later I was walking down Fifty-seventh Street with my same pink-and-green shirtwaist dress on, carrying my same portfolio and the same thing happened again and I made the same mistake. I could have killed myself. Nobody could be that dumb. This very handsome young man rushed up to me. "Ann?" "No—" "Oh, excuse me, I'm so sorry. I am so embarrassed— I could've sworn your name was Ann." I fell for it, laughing, "No, I'm Maggie." He snapped his fingers. "Oh, of course, Maggie. How could I have forgotten. I am so glad to see you again. How've you been? How's your boy friend?" I fell right into it. "We're married now." And I was studying his face and trying to remember where I'd met him. "Yes, of course. Guess I'm absentminded today. You know, you did a marvelous audition." "Where?" "Over at NBC." I was giving him all the lines, stupid me. "I didn't audition at NBC, I auditioned at CBS." "Oh, right. Well, I see so many auditions I guess I get mixed up sometimes. How are your folks?" "They're fine." "You know, I'm from North Carolina." (I guess he caught the accent.) "I'm an agent now and I'm doing very well. I would love to see what I can do for you because you were really great that day." I kept trying to remember who was there that day and I could not for the life of me recall seeing him, but I had been very nervous so I thought I just hadn't noticed him. "Can you come up to my office? Do you have pictures?" "Yes," and I held up my portfolio.

"Do you have time now?" "Yes." "Well, come on. We can take a short cut through this drugstore." Fine. Why not? So we went through the drugstore. Actually, we were going to his hotel room and he wanted to fool me by going through the drugstore. We go up the service elevator and we go in and it's a bedroom. "This is your office?" He was very personable. "Yes, what would you have to drink?" I was mad. "I won't drink anything." "Don't you drink?" "Yes." I was so furious I wasn't scared. "But not when I'm at a meeting. A *business* meeting. Well? Do you want my pictures or not?" "In a minute," and he turned down the light and put on the radio and flipped up my skirt. I slapped him hard in the face, picked up my portfolio, ran for the door and zipped open my portfolio, sailed a couple of pictures at him and stormed out. "If you want to know more about me, contact my husband. Or better yet, I'll have him contact you! Right in the teeth!"

My pictures were falling out as I started down the hall and the maid passed me by with that tisk, tisk look like, "Another one." I was so mad at myself I could have cut my own throat. *You fool, you fool, you fool*, I thought, all the way home. *That's twice in two weeks!*

After that, when I walked down Fifty-seventh Street I walked like a New Yorker. I didn't look to the right or to the left and I certainly did not look at people. It was looking right into the faces of people that got me in trouble. I walked straight ahead like I really knew where I was going and people would think, *There goes a girl with a purpose*. It worked. I never got picked up again.

I found a small modeling agency, rather on the shabby side, but it was an agency, wasn't it? and they gave me work immediately. It was more work getting away from the photographers than posing for them. I don't know anything about astrology, but brother, the planet Saturn must've been big in my chart for the season.

The photographers would usually start out behaving and pose me for "nice" pictures. They would then come on strong. Things like, "Would you like to make some extra money?" "How?"

"Some nude pictures?" "Oh, no!" "Well, there's nothing wrong with it." "I know, but I don't want to." They have different approaches, but their motives were all the same. After my firm refusal the door leading out usually became difficult to reach and harder to open. Some of these creeps would bar the door and try to con me into staying. Others would grab at my bust thinking their touch would send me into a swoon, no doubt, as I kicked in a few shins. My backside often had pinch marks on it. I kicked more men, slapped more men that year than ever before and certainly ever since. I usually left them in a state of shock because I didn't look the type to belt anybody.

One man, a very good photographer, took loads of marvelous pictures. Wonderful action shots, but the action hadn't begun yet. When he finished shooting, I was in the dressing room, changing into street wear and he stuck his head in. "Can I see something?" "What?" "Any place, any part of you." "Any place, any part of me? Here's my elbow!" "No. I want to see the places you've got covered up." "No!" "Would you kiss me?" "No!" "Why? Because I'm Jewish?" "That has nothing to do with it." So I called his bluff and kissed him on the cheek. "How's that? Good-bye. I'll send my husband over to pick up my pictures." Bill didn't think the free pictures were worth a free-for-all so he wouldn't go back for them.

There was another place Bill was reluctant to go to: church. And I didn't want to go unless he went with me. I realize, now that I look back, he was just too tired on a Sunday morning after working as a waiter all night, but I nagged and nagged until the poor thing finally gave in. After two trials we gave up.

The first Sunday that I managed to have the upper hand, with Bill fussing and grumbling all the way, we went to a church around the corner from where we lived. The entire sermon was in German. Bill grinned a lot on the way home. The next Sunday we tried another church a couple of blocks away. A lady got up in a long pink evening dress and started reading from a book. I thought, *My goodness, its only twelve thirty in the afternoon, what is the lady doing in an evening dress?* It seemed very peculiar to be in a church without a preacher. Bill laughed a lot on the way home.

After that "Would you kiss me?" episode Bill and I agreed enough was enough. I would just have to concentrate on acting and skip the bread-and-butter modeling money. It wasn't worth it. The Muses were kind. Just after our decision that I quit trying to model, Bill got a part in the Broadway show *The World of Suzie Wong*. I was so happy that he got the first acting job because he was the husband. I thought it would help secure our insecure marriage. Instead, I became jealous of all those gorgeous Oriental girls he worked with. He would show me how they gave him an Oriental back rub and the way he talked about them, I knew he dug them. When he went on the road with the show I was very upset. All I could think of was those girls stroking Bill's back.

My birthday came around and I waited all day for a present from Bill. Nothing came. No card, no gift, no call. I was very depressed and I had a voice lesson that afternoon so I went next door to my neighbor's and asked her if she would listen out for my doorbell because I was expecting a present and she said she would, so, confident that the gift would come, I left to keep my lesson with Colin Romoff.

After my lesson I said, "Today is my birthday." He said, "Is it really? What are you and your husband going to do today?" I said, "Well, he's out of town." And tears started in my eyes. I bit my lip and gulped a lot. "You poor child." He made me feel sorry for myself and I snapped, "Oh, that's all right. Bill won't forget." He said, "You sweet thing. What is your address?" I know Colin had the best of intentions. He was probably going to send me flowers or something, but he forgot.

I went home and I waited. It was still early and I just knew Bill wouldn't let my birthday go by. The phone rang and I raced for it. It would be Bill, of course. It was Dasheila, my friend from North Carolina who had also studied at the Playhouse. "Maggie, I know today is your birthday and since Bill is out of town I think we should celebrate. Let's have tea." Dasheila was very proper. She came over and brought me a lovely present, a *fleur de lis* pin which I still wear often. We had tea, she wished me a happy birthday and left.

I washed the cups and saucers and sat by the window hoping

to see a mailman bringing a present for me. It was a cold day and the sun was barely breaking through the heavy smog above. There was no mailman. I brooded all day.

That night I got out the presents my parents had sent a few days earlier which I had not yet opened, as I wanted to open them when I got Bill's. I stuck a candle in a cupcake and lit the candle and sang Happy Birthday, Dear Me. I made a wish (that Bill would send me a present), blew out the candle and sat on the bed, pretending I had company, and opened my gifts. No joke, I talked to my imaginary guests. "Oh, look, this is from Mother—" and I would hold it up and talk about it. I did that with all of them. After my party I really felt lonely. At two o'clock that morning I couldn't stand it any longer so I called Bill in Philadelphia. He was out. I panicked. I thought maybe he was ill and that would explain why he hadn't sent me a card or anything. I kept calling back every half hour and finally I fell asleep. About five that morning I got a call from him. "What the hell have you been calling me for?" I said, "Today is my birthday." "Oh, Lord, Maggie. . . . Can you forgive me?" He explained how hard they were working and that night he had gone out with some of the boys. He really felt awful. Two days later I got a card from him. Real cute. A little housewife was on the front, pushing a grocery cart!

When he came home and they opened in New York, we started looking for a bigger apartment. We agreed that part of our problem in getting along might be the confining quarters. Being in one room with no place, except the bathroom, to get away from each other, might be getting on our nerves. If we had lived in the Taj Mahal it would have been the same situation, but I didn't face that fact until I had no choice but to look at the truth.

Soon after, we moved to a bigger apartment. And soon after, Bill quit his show. I guess he was hoping to get a bigger part in another show. When he left, he just moped around and looked miserable. I had gotten a job in an off-Broadway production called *Many Loves*. It was not an Equity cast, but I was guaranteed forty-five dollars a week. It was three short plays and I had the lead in the second one. This was a repertory company so everybody got paid the same amount, even the little boy who came in at the last of the three plays to say, "Mama." After a few weeks they wanted to cut my salary down to ten dollars a week.

The night I came home with the bad news Bill flew into a rage. "They can't do that to you! You're too good. You're great in that part." He went to that phone and he called them and really gave them what for. "You don't realize the talent you've got and you want to pay her ten dollars a week? She is not going to work for you as of this moment. She is too good and she has gotten fantastic reviews for you. Don't pay that kid! He's got one line!" And they said, "Oh, but we thought Eileen (I changed my name to Eileen Fulton when I got that show) was in this for the love of art." Bill yelled, "She loves it, but she deserves to get paid for it." I was so proud to hear him take up for me like that. So, after all the blasting Bill gave them they agreed to pay me twenty dollars a week. I wanted to act and at least the money paid for my transportation back and forth.

One night after I came home from a performance, I took a good look at my sad-faced husband and I said, "Bill, why don't you go away? Take a vacation from me." He looked at me with deep appreciation. "I was hoping you would say that because that's what I want to do."

He left on the *Queen Mary* a few days later for Europe. I realized that day he would not miss me. I also realized I was relieved to see him go.

It was summer when he sailed away. I decided to take advantage of the free time I would have and take up my search for an agent. But summer is not the most ideal time of the year to try to get one. Still, I was determined. I would nail him to the chair and make him listen to me if I had to.

The way I got one of the best agents in New York was not by nailing him to the chair but by kicking his door down.

It was on a Friday and, in the summer, most offices close for a longer weekend. It was hot as blazes that day and several times my feet begged me to take them home, but something wouldn't let me give up so I kept walking. By the time I reached William

McCaffrey's office, I was a bit wilted, but that hot sun had acted as a charge. I knocked at Mr. McCaffrey's door and heard people talking, but no one would answer. I knocked a few more times— no one would respond. They were laughing now. I got mad. It was like, "We hear ya knockin' but ya can't come in." I backed off and gave that door a severe kick and—it fell in. So did I. I skidded in on my fanny, my pictures flying everywhere. I learned later the door was off its hinges. It was being repaired.

A man jumped up from a chair and shouted angrily, "Who the hell are you?" "I'm an actress!" I yelled back, scrambling to my feet and collecting my pictures. "Who the hell are you?" He laughed and the two women, his receptionist and secretary who were on a lunch break, laughed too. I didn't. That purple-eyed dragon in me was ready to extinguish them. "I'm an actress and I need an agent!" They stopped laughing. He smiled. "With an entrance like that, you've got one." That was the beginning of my career and a long friendship with a wonderful man.

My first job was doing *Blue Denim* in Mount Kisco, New York. When I auditioned for the part, I didn't tell the producer I was married for fear they would think I wasn't young enough to play the role so, when my wedding anniversary began to draw near, I started haunting the mailbox every day looking for a present from Bill. After forgetting my birthday, he just couldn't forget our anniversary, but he did. It didn't make sense because Bill was so thoughtful all during the year with sudden unexpected presents for no reason at all.

The night of our anniversary I was very depressed. People in the company sensed something was wrong, but I couldn't tell anyone I was married. I was so afraid I would get fired, which was ridiculous, but a lot of things I thought and did were ridiculous in those days.

One of the set designers felt sorry for me I guess and asked me to have dinner with him. He wasn't trying to get fresh or anything, he was just being nice to ol' droopy-looking me. He took me out to a lovely restaurant and after we ordered he said, "What's wrong, Eileen? Something is bothering you, now what is it?" Oh, how I wanted to tell him it was my anniversary and Bill had forgotten, but I knew I would cry so I acted silly and giddy and when he ordered wine with our meal, I really got silly and giddy. I didn't drink often. Sometimes I would have a beer or two. But the wine brought back the recollection of my first taste. It was in a church. I can't remember the denomination because I got stoned on the wine.

It was during the Apple Festival when we were living in Mooresville. I was one of the beauty contest winners and about six of us were invited to attend the world-wide communion. I discovered we were being served wine, which is not done in the Methodist Church. I had been taught all my life that drinking liquor is a sin so I couldn't understand the contradiction. Here I was in a church getting wine free. I was so curious about the taste that when the single cup was passed to me I took a big swallow to wash away any germs since drinking after people was supposed to be unsanitary and that big swallow brought on a terrible case of the hiccups. All the kids got the giggles as did I. I knew it was disrespectful, but the more I tried not to, the more giggly I got. Everybody turned around and tutted and that made us want to laugh all the more. They looked me up and down like, *You've won a contest, you're grown-up, you should be ashamed.* My head was throbbing and I was trying to hold my breath so I bit my glove until my teeth ached, but the hiccups just kept on coming. I hadn't had any breakfast so I thought I must be drunk since drunks hiccup.

Thinking about that Apple Festival made me silly, as I said, when our wine was served that night and I guess he thought he had made a big mistake to think I was unhappy about something.

When *Blue Denim* closed I went back to New York full of grand resolutions to put our marriage back together again, but like Humpty Dumpty it was doomed. But I gave it a good go before I called it quits.

Since we had moved into the new apartment we had done very little about fixing it up. Our wedding presents were still packed since the day we got married because Bill wouldn't let me open them. Two weeks before Bill was due in I opened every one of the presents, made drapes and didn't do too badly considering I can't sew very well. I bought a nine-foot pole to hang them on and since I couldn't get it on a bus or a subway I walked the fifteen blocks home with it over my shoulder. I met a lot of people along the way who wanted to help me with it. By the time I dragged it home, that pole and I had become good friends. (I still have it. I can't use it, but it's under my bed and I'm forever stubbing my toe on it. Someday I just might have a nine-foot-wide window and can make use of it.)

On the day Bill was due in, I bought flowers for the house, got myself all dolled up, piled my hair on top of my head to make me look older, more sophisticated, made a daiquiri for him which was his favorite drink, stuck it in the refrigerator to keep it cool and waited for my beloved.

When he called that afternoon, he sounded exhausted. "I'm at the East Side Terminal. I'll be home soon." I figured it would take him about twenty minutes. Three hours later he arrived. He came in tired and bored. He thought the apartment looked nice, I looked nice, the daiquiri was nice and he fell asleep where he sat.

Bill brought a lot of beautiful gifts for me, but I knew it was over.

The next night Bill went out with one of our friends from the Playhouse and around three that morning he called and said he was in jail and that's why he hadn't come home. My Bill in jail! I nearly died. "What for?" "Well, I got mad at this bus driver because he closed the door in John's face and I said to him, 'Why did you do that?' and the driver said, 'Because I felt like it!' so I grabbed his money changer and slammed it to the floor and said, 'Well, I feel like doing this!' and the driver started yelling for the cops so we ran. The cops chased us with guns and hollered for us to stop so when we saw the guns we surrendered. So, I'm in jail." I said, very calmly, very wisely, "Now, Bill, this will be a marvelous experience for you as an actor. You observe every-thing that you see because this is something you could never ask for. Make use of being in jail because something good can come from it." That's how I have always felt about everything that happened to me. As an actress, I could use the experience. When we got divorced, I thought, *This is something I must remember. When a part comes along as a divorcee I will know how to handle it. I will remember how I felt and use it.* That's why I can play the role of a mother on my show because I took care of my younger brothers.

After Bill explained everything, the police let them out of jail. The next day was a holiday. It was Labor Day weekend. Bill and I had a terrible fight that afternoon. I ran in the bathroom crying and screaming and he ran in after me and kicked the door shut and we screamed and yelled at each other calling each other terrible names. We yelled into each other's face until we were deaf. I became hysterical and he turned calm and picked up a little glass, filled it with water slowly and splash, threw it in my face. I guess he thought that would just fix me right up. That made me madder and I grabbed the doorknob but the door wouldn't open. Somehow, it had locked from the outside when he kicked it shut. Our fight was over. Bill pulled and pulled the doorknob. We were locked in.

Bill went to the window and looked down to call for help. Two stories below a group of people stood staring up at Bill expecting to witness a murder. Our private war had become a public spectacle. Bill stepped back, embarrassed. "Maggie, we've got an audience I'm afraid." "Ohh, I bet they heard everything we said!" We laughed but not for long. We tried the door again. Bill went back to the window and yelled, "Would someone please get our doorman and tell him we're locked in the bathroom?" Those jerks just stood there grinning at us. They wouldn't do a thing. I guess they thought we were drunk. Bill yelled again for them to call the doorman. Somebody finally got him and he called up to say he didn't have a passkey to our apartment and the superintendent was away for the holiday so it was tough luck for us, we would have to spend the weekend in the bathroom. We were doomed to nothing but toothpaste and water. Bill asked the viewers to throw up a hammer. Minutes later a hammer sailed up and Bill caught it, but it didn't do us any good. There was a big mirror on the door and we were afraid to bang in case the glass shattered. Finally the doorman said he wasn't spending his weekend tossing up sandwiches and he disappeared.

I sat on the floor and cried and Bill looked like he might join me any minute. Then came the most beautiful sound we had ever heard. A key in the bathroom door. Freedom! We instantly resumed our mad. I clutched at my robe and like a streak of lightning raced past the poor doorman, who stood holding his torn pants.

He had had to break into the superintendent's apartment to get the passkey and in the process of breaking the law he tore his pants. I got into my clothes and got out a needle and sewed up our savior's pants.

The next day Bill said, "Maggie, your birthday is coming up and it is only fair that since I took a vacation that you have a change, too. Why don't you take a couple of weeks somewhere?" That sounded like a great idea. After that awful fight, I needed a break. I had heard of a beautiful place called Lake Minnewaska in upstate New York so I decided I would go. I loved the mountains and they had never failed to give me a sense of peace which was something I hadn't felt for a long time. I asked Bill to go with me. He wouldn't. So I went.

I had a wonderful time. I felt relaxed for the first time since I married Bill. The woods were magnificent. Fall was coming and there is nothing so beautiful, so exhilarating as the fall. I did a lot of thinking and under the influence of the woods, the lake, the cliffs, I realized there was nothing so wonderful about our marriage. I could not deceive myself any longer. We were not right for each other and all we had been doing was prolonging the agony of a divorce. Yet, I knew I didn't have the courage to tell him.

I stayed away a week and when I came home, I walked right into a job working with a man I had wanted to work with for a long time—Alan Schneider. It was a big off-Broadway production, *Summer of the Seventeenth Doll.* A few days later, as I came home from rehearsal, Bill met me in the foyer with a towel around his waist. He said, "Maggie, I don't know how to tell you this, but I'm afraid when I was in Europe I got crabs in one of those hotel rooms." "Really? Were there any lobsters, too?" He seemed very exasperated. "You fool! Don't you know what crabs are?" "Crabs? Well, sure—were they soft shell or what? You mean they were in the room with you?" He was nearing the point of no return. "My God. They were in the room with me and now they're on my body." I got the picture. I had heard of body lice but I'd never heard of crabs.

I remembered one time when I was a child and our teacher gave us a lecture about lice. If you came near a child who scratched his head too much, you were supposed to run from him so you wouldn't get them in your hair. The teacher said, "Now children, it is not a disgrace to get lice, it is only a disgrace to keep them."

Bill told me what to do and the treatment began. I only had one so I wasn't a disgrace for long, but I was furious with him for sitting on one of those foreign johns and catching them. Well, it was another experience. A few days later my agent submitted my name for a part in a television serial. The part was that of a Southern white-trash girl. And I thought, *Boy, can I play this part. I've had something all white-trash people get!* Of course I was over it, but I used the experience and got the role. I was to go in rehearsal the same day *Summer of the Seventeeth Doll* opened and I became afraid I couldn't do both. Like a fool I quit because at that time I didn't know my capacity for work. How I have regretted it because it was a marvelous part and would have helped me out of the "sweet, young girl" role I was always playing.

One afternoon I was looking through Bill's files as I wanted to see some of our old honeymoon pictures and he got furious because I had my fingers in his files. He started screaming and shouting about not having any privacy and bouncing things around and I got mad and ran in the kitchen and picked up a pot and cracked him over the head.

I've still got the pot with the dent in it to prove it. We went screaming around the house like a couple of halfwits. I cried, "I wish you were dead! Oh, how I wish you were dead!" Suddenly I came to my senses and I thought, *God, I don't wish him dead. What's the matter with me? Have I gone crazy?* So I ran out to the kitchen to cool down and I sat in a chair and said, "Bill, I want a divorce." He rubbed his sore head and nodded. "You said it. I didn't." That night when I came home from rehearsal I found him packing.

When I came in, I guess he didn't hear me because he was playing a record that we had loved from a musical we had seen together and I heard him cry. I went to him and put my arms around him. There was no hate in us anymore. There was only what had always been between us—friendship. Bill and I were never meant to be lovers and we both knew it now. I said, "Bill, you don't have to leave like this. Wait until you find a place." He held me out from him and looked at me the way he used to when we first met. "I really think it best because I don't want to hurt you and I get so mad at you that I might." We just stood there being ourselves for the first time and being sorry.

The next day our show, *Summer of the Seventeenth Doll*, had moved to a new theater in the Bowery. Quite a comedown from the theater we were in before, but the house was booked out so we took what we could get. The neighborhood was rough, but that didn't bother me at all. I was acting. That's the only thing that has ever mattered—then and now. But I was mortally upset about the divorce and while backstage I was suddenly overcome with self-pity and cried into the curtain. Alan Schneider came over to me. "Eileen, what's wrong?" I told him I was getting divorced, but I didn't want anybody in the cast to know. He said, "The best cure for pain is work. So put your soul into this show. Work, Eileen, work."

He must have talked with one of the girls in the cast because the night, during a rehearsal, Themis, the girl, asked if I would like to have dinner at her house. I gratefully accepted because I couldn't face going out to dinner alone with only my thoughts for company. Alan must have told her about the divorce because she and her husband prepared a feast. We had stuffed mushrooms, avocado salad, a beautiful dinner. They were so kind and attentive; they had to know something was bothering me. I think they saved me that night. I was really depressed.

The next day I knew I had to call Mother before she heard the bad news some other way. I did not know what kind of response I would get, but she was wonderful. So sweet and sympathetic. None of that, "Can't you try to work it out?" And I wasn't the preacher's daughter being held up as an example. It was a mother talking to her only daughter whom she loved and was concerned for. That was her only thought. "Are you all right? What can we do to help?"

She told Daddy that night and she said he grew very pale and shook his head saying, "I've helped other people with their problems and I can't help my own daughter."

Thanksgiving Day Bill and I got a legal separation. We met very properly and then we went out for dinner to celebrate our separation. He was very nice, and our time together went by pleasantly. He told me he was going to California to see what sort of work he could get on the West Coast. I had a show to do so we parted outside the restaurant. As we walked away in opposite directions a great sense of loneliness settled over me. Bill was going far away to that place I had dreamed of as a child. As I walked toward the theater suddenly I began to feel alive again. I remember seeing things, seeing birds, the sky, the faces of people—I was lonely, yes, but it was the kind of loneliness that says, Look! there's room now in this emptiness to expand, to love again, to grow and learn from this experience with Bill. I began to run, darting around people who turned to stare after me. I didn't care what people thought. I had a new life waiting for me and I didn't intend to keep destiny locked and bolted a minute longer.

I have always been a hard worker, but as of that night, I gave every performance, every person I met, everything I did, all of myself. I wanted to have friends, go places, do things because I had not allowed myself to do anything but work until that time. I wanted to live with every fiber of my being, to really *feel*, because that's what life is all about.

A few days later I received a letter from my parents saying they were going to take turns coming to New York to visit me. Mother came the first week. She went to see the show every night. She was so thrilled and proud when people in the audience would talk about me. "That young girl is very good." Mother would beam and say, "That's my daughter." She was very distressed though about my working in the Bowery and insisted after she left I have someone walk with me until I got a cab.

Christmas Day Mother got out all the silver and polished everything. Sewed up all my things, bleached out my underwear, cleaned out Bill's drawers, a task I could not bring myself to do. She did all the dirty work and we had our own Christmas party, just the two of us.

I was kind of sobby and Bill was on my mind constantly. I hoped he was having a nice holiday wherever he was and then he called. Was I all right? Did I need any money? Was I getting along okay? That was the real Bill. The boy I thought I had fallen in love with when we were students at the Playhouse. I told him Mother was with me and I didn't need anything, thank you. I wished him a "merry" and a "happy." When I hung up, I looked around the apartment and thought how wise Bill had been to move out right away. We had prolonged the agony long enough. Somehow, that call really made our break final.

My World in Pictures

One year old and already I loved to have my picture taken.

My second birthday party. Even then I would not put down the treasured phone.

The day I ate the Ivory soap but naturally I recovered completely for the camera.

A very happy child. Uncle Tokie had just brought me my dog Mickey.

UPPER LEFT: *Mickey (wrapped in a baby blanket) in my lap recovering from the overfeeding I had given her.* UPPER RIGHT: *Mickey, a year later, learning to walk on hind legs.*

Perched on a piano stool I model the evening dress I had borrowed from my mother for my surprise visit to Church when Grand Daddy was preaching on following in one's parent's foot steps.

Grand Daddy McLarty.

I don't know who loved
snow more—Mickey or
me! We both ate it!

Nanny, my grandmother, takes me to visit my mother in the hospital. Mother had knitted both our coats.

The day Mother and Daddy accidentally left me alone at the beach. Look—No teeth!

LEFT: Off to Hollywood. RIGHT: One of my costumes for talking to the flowers.

My first evening dress. The yellow polka dot one which mother and I couldn't resist though it cost nine dollars.

And my all-girl birthday at which I wore it.

The minister and his wife on a walk with little Miss Priss–Prim.

Our first day at Staten Island we visited Daddy's ship.

LEFT: *As Mistress Mary in a piano recital in Belmont.* RIGHT: *Playing desperado with my Uncle Tokie.*

On my way to my first opera.

And the next April at Palisades Park. I was dreaming of Jerry Johnson.

LEFT: *A hot summer on Staten Island. The baby is my brother Jimmy.* RIGHT: *Outside the Charles Addams house we first lived in at Marion—the one with the rats in the backyard.*

For my thirteenth birthday Mother bought me a crown of gold and silver sequins. Perhaps because after my display at the opera she had told me to "take off my crown."

LEFT: *With Jimmy in front of Daddy's Church there.* RIGHT: *Elizabeth Cross and I build our Venus de Milo.*

The house the congregation built for us in Marion.

Dressed for my 16th birthday party and ready and waiting for the presents.

BELOW LEFT: *On my way to Camp South Toe.* BELOW MIDDLE: *And the day I was so proud of cleaning the kerosene lanterns there. Not exactly understanding what a latrine was.* BELOW RIGHT: *The handsome blue coat Elizabeth Cross gave me.*

My little mother role. Taking care of my brothers Charles and Jimmy was often fun.

Mother and myself outside our house in Mooresville the day she had to stand inspection by a committee of the congregation.

Charles and Jimmy who had caused all the commotion surrounded by my mother and myself. They look pleased with themselves!

In our high school production of "Oh, Susanna."

After I got a black eye
from a hard driven ten-
nis ball of my swain's I
experimented with tough
roles. The next Sunday
for Church I wore what
I imagined was a French
tart's outfit. It not only
captured him, but it also
captured my part in "A
Girl of the Night" years
later. This is more or less
how I dressed for that
audition.

After we were graduated my friend Nonnie and I stripped off our hot robes to the bathing suits we'd been wearing underneath.

LEFT: *In the dressing room for "Lost Colony"—my very first job after college.* RIGHT: *Here I'm singing "Shortnin' Bread" in a musical review in North Carolina. My mother later sent this snap to my father-in-law-to-be to let him know what was coming into his family.*

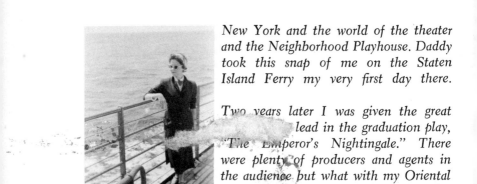

New York and the world of the theater and the Neighborhood Playhouse. Daddy took this snap of me on the Staten Island Ferry my very first day there.

Two years later I was given the great lead in the graduation play, "The Emperor's Nightingale." There were plenty of producers and agents in the audience but what with my Oriental make up I might as well have been invisible. No jobs. That's me in the middle.

Me and my wedding dress. Taken for the newspapers.

BELOW LEFT AND CENTER: *Snaps of Bill's on our honeymoon. In the decolletage one he'd been so quiet I looked out to see what he was doing and was caught.* BELOW RIGHT: *Our first move— "Help."*

LEFT: *My first picture that I gave to agents. It was a regular snapshot. I didn't know what an 8x10 was.* RIGHT: *Bill took this when I was on my way to my very first audition. The producer was Helen Wagner's (Nancy Hughes) husband in real life, but I didn't know that then.*

A most dramatic moment for True Story Magazine. (Real tears!)
At one time they had me hanging from a cliff—literally.

A scene in "The Summer of the
Seventeenth Doll."

With Richard Fithian
in "Blue Denim."

LEFT: *This was taken the day after Bill and I parted.* RIGHT: *In the first months on "As the World Turns" Ted Cordey often had me in tears.*

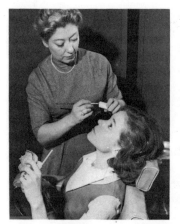 

LEFT: *June Gossett our makeup woman would repair the damage.*
RIGHT: *When I was telling Nancy that I was pregnant and married to Bob.*

And John Conboy stage manager, could always cheer me up.

And with Bob (Don Hastings) after I had moved into the Hughes home. Grandpa's eagle is on the wall. (We referred to the bedroom as the bordello.)

With Nancy (Helen Wagner) in the Hughes livingroom.

My "ugly" picture of my Hell Burner days. This one got me many jobs.

Making up for the movie "Girl of the Night" with Anne Francis and Kay Medford.

A high moment in "Girl of the Night." I was moving so fast I was a blur.

LEFT: *I came home to a real, honest-to-goodness surprise party my mother had engineered before the opening of "Girl of the Night." RIGHT: With my little brother, Charles, Barbara Davis of "World" and Ronnie Welch who had been my first Bob Hughes, at the premiere of "Girl of the Night."*

At home with Ginger before I had to send her back to North Carolina.

Breakfast and the script for "World." This was for the magazine piece which didn't sell because my life was "too unglamorous" and real.

But at the photographer's insistence I did whistle down a cab instead of taking the usual bus.

On the set with Chris Hughes (Don McLaughlin) that day.

Helen Wagner (Nancy) and Frankie . Michaels (Tom) and I celebrate "World Turn" 9th birthday.

Our communal dressing room at "Fantasticks."

After the show Patsy Bruder of "World" and her husband came back stage. I've always done that with my skirt when I'm happy. Remember when I got Mickey?

With Henderson For-
sythe in "Who's
Afraid of Virginia
Woolf." A very dif-
ferent role for him
from his "World"
one of a kindly doctor.

I finally squeaked out High F with my voice teacher Bernard Taylor beaming at me.

With Henry Fanelli, my harpist for a singing date.

Catching my own dinner in Galveston when I was at the Balinese Room. I caught, and Adolph, the chef who was so kind to me, cooked.

Under Helen Wagner's (Nancy Hughes) guidance I get interested in real cooking.

Michael Avedon took this publicity shot of me on my terrace. It was for promoting the more glamorous Lisa in the short-lived, night time show, "Our Private World" and for wearing Sara Coventry Jewelry while doing it!

With Tom Poston in "The Owl and the Pussycat" in Guy
Little's Theatre. This was the run we barely survived what with
throwing a heavy t.v. set at each other and coming down with the
Hong Kong flu.

With my manager, Dori Davis. Me in my first mink coat.

Kidding around with Guy Little on the day of my wonderful birthday party—or parties.

My first day back at "World" (January 16, 1967 after being away a year) as the New Lisa.

With Grandpa Hughes (Santos Ortega).

I tell Claire Shea (Barbara Berger) that I am going to have a child by her husband.

My present living room opening on the terrace. Now I feel I really have a home.

With Amelia Earhart in the foyer of my present apartment.

And I love my kitchen.

Getting ready for a party.

This is dear Frankie who selects and sells me all of my clothes, from night club gowns to slack suits. (Most have been worn on "World")

Amelia and I study next day's script.

On the set in Lisa's living room. You can see I wear my own clothes as Lisa. My brother Jimmy took this picture.

A wonderful meeting with my parents at the airport when I flew down to North Carolina to buy the house.

7

Not long after Mother left, Daddy, who was then a commander in the Naval Reserve, had a two-week tour of duty so he came to see me, but I didn't know exactly when he was coming. It was to be a surprise.

The night Daddy arrived I had two shows to do so it was 1:00 A.M. when I got home. The doorman, who had become very protective of me since the day he tore his pants to get Bill and me out of the bathroom, stopped me and very mysteriously said, "A man in uniform came here and he claims he's your father. I saw the chaplain insignia so I thought it might be all right to let him into your place. Your father a chaplain?" I laughed and told him yes. "I'm going up with you and wait till you tell me it's him."

He went up with me and I tiptoed in to find my sweet daddy asleep on the couch. I nodded to the doorman and he waved and left. I looked down at Daddy and wanted desperately to wake him, but I knew he must be tired or he would have called the theater. I gave up my nightly bath because I didn't want the noise of water running to disturb him so I quietly got ready for bed. He must have felt my presence because I hadn't been under the covers a minute when he came in and put his arm under my head and gave me a big hug. No words, he just squeezed me very tight and went back in the living room. A lifetime of love flooded my being in that unspoken moment. He told me volumes of words without the need of any.

Daddy stayed a week and it was a beautiful slice of time for both of us. That first day I took him to the theater. He looked so handsome in his uniform and that slow, warm smile of his knocked everybody out. One of the kids said, "For a minister he's pretty groovy." True. He doesn't use sugar or saccharine on people. He's a hand shaker, not a "God bless you, brother" back slapper.

While I was doing a matinee that day he went grocery shopping and filled my shelves. All I had in the house when he arrived was a bag of grits, a can of peas and a can of hash. At that time I was still very frugal and lived on grits as a major portion of my diet. He bought lots of steaks, which was a luxury I had never allowed myself, and he insisted on doing most of the cooking. We really got to know each other in that week and we spent every free hour talking about anything and everything—except Bill.

He drove me to and from the theater every night and during the day, made rounds with me. It was a fun experience for him and relieved his worries about lecherous old men behind big desks. He wanted to know what my life was like and it was my pleasure to show him. He accompanied me on my appointments for auditions, commercials and television interviews. He also met my agent, Mr. McCaffrey, whom he liked instantly. Partly because Mr. McCaffrey treated me like his daughter, which pleased Daddy very much.

During the entire week the oddest thing kept happening: Wherever we would go, I would bump into people I knew. I had walked around Manhattan for months on end when I was alone without seeing a single person I knew and, suddenly, it was like they were all being drawn to me like a magnet. Daddy was beginning to think life in New York was no different from a small town where everybody knows everybody.

Just before he left, he stocked my shelves again. Our last day together was a quiet one. He didn't bring up the subject of the divorce, but I knew he was waiting for me to talk about it and I just couldn't. I didn't want to end his visit in tears. His eyes were asking me to trust him, to talk to him whenever I felt I could and when he said good-bye he gave me a hug, "Old Girl, I'm proud of you." When he walked away he left more than shelves stocked with food, he left me love.

That spring, *Summer of the Seventeenth Doll* closed and I got a small part in a Broadway show, *One for the Dame*. And I got the part by fighting for it. The day I auditioned, before I read, I went up to meet the producer, the director and the writer. They looked me over and said, "Thank you very much, leave your pictures here." I said, "When will the reading be?" "There won't be a reading. You're not right for the part." I almost cried. "Why?" "You're too pretty." I joyously announced the miracle of the day. "I can be very homely," and ripped off my false eyelashes, scrubbed off my lipstick, slapped my hands to my head, pressing down my hair, "See? See how homely I am?" They were hysterical and thought that was quite a performance. They gave me a script and told me to come back the next day and read.

The next day (after I'd practically memorized the whole script) I read and, very big-eyed, I asked, "Have I got it?" In unison they said, "Yes." The character I was to portray was a little girl who played the violin and thought she was pregnant but instead she had the measles.

When I got the part, I was so afraid ever to be caught looking pretty for fear they would fire me on the spot, that I started wearing jeans and old shirts of Bill's. No make-up other than lipstick, and I whacked off my hair. There were ten men in the show and since I dressed like a boy, they treated me like one, which bothered me terribly, but I didn't know what else to do about my looks. It was very depressing to be homely all the time, but that job meant everything o me.

It was a comedy starring Richard Whorf. His son David was in it too. I played the part of David's homely girl friend, Nancy. The show was set for Broadway but we didn't make it. We rehearsed in the Bowery at a theater that was crawling with rats and freezing cold. I was beginning to think I would never get out of the Bowery, having played *Summer* there just before I got this part.

Even though it was a tiny part, it was mine to do and make the most of. The stagehands didn't understand how important it was to me and when I would prepare for my scene, I demanded absolute silence backstage. They would get annoyed with me acting like "the star" so they played a joke on me one day. I had requested from the very first day that my violin case be weighted so I could carry it more realistically. But when the jokers put a sandbag in the case and I reached for the case, the only thing that came off the ground was me. I was livid. "Get that thing out of my case." They just stood there and laughed, but their grins vanished when I got through with them. "This is no way to act in the professional theater! Where do you think you are?" When they realized how seriously I took my work, they apologized and never disturbed me again when I was preparing for my gem of a scene.

The few times I would risk looking pretty were when my new boy friend would fly out to see me. It was a beautiful affair of the mind. I met him just before I got the show and he was everything Bill was not. He loved opera, concerts, poetry and he loved to sing. He was a romanticist and I thought I was in love with him. He almost killed me on Valentine's Day so I stopped dating him for one day and when I went on the road he kept flying out to see me and, well, what girl isn't flattered by that?

But that Valentine's Day we went to a party up in Westchester County somewhere and it was bitter cold. I had not wanted to go because I had an audition the next morning for a Broadway show and I wanted to be rested, but John insisted. He borrowed his brother's car and we went. Now, John usually didn't drink very much, but the night of the party, he got smashed. I didn't realize how high he was until we started to go home. When I saw him stagger, I panicked. I couldn't drive because I had let my license expire and he was in no condition to get behind the wheel, but it was freezing out. My little thin evening shoes and thin evening coat were no protection against the wind and snow. I had two alternatives: freeze to death on the sidewalk or risk getting killed in the car. The car at least would be warm. And maybe he would somehow manage. As I was helping him in this handsome Argentinian who had been at the party came up to us and said, "Eileen, I must come with you because I don't think John is able to handle himself." I looked at that gorgeous hunk of man and sighed like Miss Helpless. I was saved. He helped John in behind the wheel, walked around and sat next to me. He couldn't drive either. I asked him what help he thought he'd be on the right side of the car since the steering wheel was on the left. Sure, he didn't want me to die alone.

John started driving and we were going onto the highway when I said hatefully, "You had better drive carefully because tomorrow I have an audition and my face better be in good condition." I hadn't finished speaking when suddenly he veered off to the left and crashed into a big supermarket. The only building near the road and he hit it. Actually, he hit a telephone pole right in front of the store. The fender was bashed in and the steering wheel would only turn to the left. John thought that very funny. "Don't worry, I know a way to go that's all left turns. I'll get you home, have no fear, John is here." So, we started going up a hill on a road that wound to the left and then the heater didn't work and the motor suddenly conked out.

John and Handsome thought this also very funny. I was burning mad but freezing to death. Then, I saw another car headed in our direction. "Here's help. Get out there and stop them." They staggered out there, acting like fools, flailing their arms up and down like scarecrows, running back and forth in the road frightening the driver so badly he crashed his car into a pole. Even I laughed. We fell in the snow, laughing on each other. Now there were two wrecked cars. This man could only make right turns and John said right turns wouldn't get us back to New York so the man chugged off going down the hill we had come up.

We got back in the car and waited and watched the deserted road like three owls on a limb. Finally we saw another car approaching. I said, "Don't you get out. I will talk to these people. I'm sober!" So, I flagged the car down and told the people I had two drunk boys with me and our car was busted and would they please take us to the nearest police station so I could get rid of them? What did I care? Those fools. They deserved a night in jail. The people laughed and said they would be glad to take us to the train. My drunk buddies piled into the car and the people gave me instructions as to what train to get back to Manhattan and there I was, holding up these two book ends. The people helped me pour them onto the train when they saw I couldn't handle them.

They slept the entire ride back and when we neared our stop, I started to leave them, but when I looked down at them, each asleep on my shoulders, they looked like children, just two drunk children and I couldn't abandon them. I gave them each a good smack and brought them around and Handsome seemed to sober up so he suggested we go to his apartment and he would fix breakfast for us. John looked green so I thought we'd better before he got sick.

The food did the trick and when John took me home he cried and said he was so sorry and I felt like some kind of a saint because he kissed the hem of my dress and I slapped him. I was such a shrew. I told him to stop being such a fool and get out and I never wanted to see him again.

The next day I applied for a driver's license and when I came home I found beautiful gardenias from John. My weakness. So, we broke up only for the night. When my show *One for the Dame* went to Boston, he was right there and often. I guess that was the most romantic time in my life. John was quite a charmer so Valentine's Day was a closed issue.

Just before the show closed in Boston, John came up and took me to dinner and we had lobster and he bought pink champagne, which I had never tasted before, and which made me laugh a lot remembering my Fifty-seventh Street pick-up scene. That night, John told me he loved me and I told him I loved him but then, soon after I returned to New York, he got a job out of town and we forgot about our eternal love.

It was at that time my rebellion began. I was suddenly bored and tired of being thought of as the sweet, adorable, feminine flower. I got out my blue jeans, bought a leather jacket and

stomped around the neighborhood in sneakers, jeans, one of Bill's
sweat shirts and the jacket. I told people around the block I was
a member of the Hell Burners. That was the name of a gang up
there. I would have dropped dead if I'd ever seen a Hell
Burner but I wanted to act tough since I had never done it
before. I was getting rid of the old and discovering the new.

I guess I acted like a child, but I had never been a child, really.
There was never a time when I could strut around in blue jeans
and act like a know-it-all. I was never allowed to get dirty so now
I deliberately made myself dirty looking. People thought I was a
hippie—I thought.

I started riding the Staten Island Ferry back and forth. I would
stay on it for hours and think and wonder what I was going to
do about my life, my attitude toward myself and other people I
had loved. I was never again going to be what other people
wanted me to be. I wanted to know what it was like to do something wild and crazy because I had never done it.

One thing I had never done was to go in a bar. I went to the
crummiest dump I could find and walked in like a cowpoke. I
didn't want to drink, I just wanted to be brave enough to go into
a joint like that. I plopped down on a stool and braced one foot
on the stool rung and nodded to the bartender. "Yes, little girl?
What can I do for you?" "I would like a drink!" Oh, I was mad.
I did not look like a little girl. "Let's see your driver's license." I
showed him. "Okay, kid, what'll you have?" "Orange juice." His
head shot forward like a rooster's. "Hunh?" He had been washing
glasses when I ordered so I said, "Oh, that's all right, you don't
have to wash a glass," thinking that was the right answer to his
startled "Hunh?" He gave me the drink, I drank it, left him a
quarter tip and walked out feeling much better. Well, I had been
in a dirty bar so I wouldn't have to do that again. It was something I had to do just to say to myself I had the courage to do it.
It was doing the opposite of what I had done. It was kind of like
going to the drugstore and sipping Cokes when I was in my teens.
Something I was not permitted to do. A minister's daughter
didn't go in drugstores and sip Cokes and flirt. She went home
and obeyed her parents. Well, I was determined to obey myself
for a change. Eileen Fulton was going to break the traditional

chains that bound her. If I was going to be proper and clean and good then it had to come because *I* chose it and not because it was expected of me. But first I had to know what it was like to be a slob. I had to see what I was missing so that I could compare. My attitude was like, *Okay, what do you think of me now! You don't like it? Too bad.*

That summer, I put away my Hell Burner outfit to go home for a week to visit my family. Mother had written saying they had gotten me a cocker spaniel. Mother had named her Virginia Dare because she was blonde and beautiful. She was six months old and a cute furry ball of butterscotch. I wasn't ready for a responsibility like that, but having something to love sounded like a wonderful idea and since she was already mine, I couldn't wait to bring her back to New York.

When I first saw her she was tied to the refrigerator door. She scrunched herself all up and started wiggling and licking as soon as I squealed at the sight of her. It was total love at first sight.

For my entire stay, Ginger, as I nicknamed her, was in my arms. She went everywhere with me, except, of course, to church. Mother told me that a dog next door had tried to mate with her but she didn't think I should worry since Ginger was only six months old.

Daddy got me a compartment for my train trip home and Ginger sat in front of the mirror looking at herself all the way back to New York. I knew then, without a doubt, we were kindred souls.

In the same week I got Ginger, I auditioned for both the Warner Brothers' movie, *Girl of the Night* and *As the World Turns.* And I got both auditions in the same way. The casting office of *Girl* had called my agent, Mr. McCaffrey, and requested a certain young actress, who must remain nameless but, fortunately for me the girl was married and about to have a baby. Caroline Allen, who handled me exclusively at the agency, told Warner Brothers about me and the audition was set up. It was a starring role and if I could get a movie, I felt my career would skyrocket.

The film was about a hippie call girl from the South and with my Southern background I thought I would be perfect. I was desperate to have a chance at portraying someone who wasn't just sweet sixteen, full of sugar and spice.

When I auditioned for the part I gave a very bad reading. I have never been able to give a good reading unless I have studied the script, but to make things worse, I had to read with the producer. There is nothing worse than trying to read a part with the man who is judging whether you are what he is looking for or not. After I finished I broke into tears and said, "I am so right for this part. I've got to have this role. Give me one more chance. Give me a couple of days and let me come back. Please— give me a script. I know how to play this girl if you will only give me another chance." He said, "Don't get your hopes up. There are about two hundred actresses in this city who are up for the part and about twenty-five of them are well known." And he named a few of them. I asked if he would mind if I brought in someone to do the scene with me and he said it would be all right. I got Dorothy Dill. She had played my mother in *Many Loves* and she was my friend so I knew I could count on her to help me.

Two days later, *As the World Turns* called the McCaffrey office asking for the actress who was pregnant and, once again, Caroline Allen told them about me and the audition was arranged. As with *Girl*, the character's name was Lisa, too. But the Lisa *World* was looking for was a nice college girl type. Certainly I knew I could play a part like that.

The audition took place at the Benton and Bowles agency. I found a room full of girls who looked very like me. They were all there to audition for the part that I wanted. I was wearing a green print shirtwaist dress which I bought for the audition at a staggering $7.50. I thought I looked the perfect plain ordinary college girl.

I was given a copy of the script thirty minutes before I read for the part. I looked at each girl as she went in and they looked as nervous as I was, but I thought the important thing here is not the lines. If I got mixed up on a line or two, okay, the important thing was to give this girl depth. There was nothing in the script to indicate what type of family Lisa came from, whether she had brothers or sisters, what she wanted out of life—nothing. So I began to make up a life for her as I sat there shaking inside, waiting for my turn.

My scene took place in a drugstore. I was to pretend to be sipping a soda with a boy named Bob Hughes, whom I hoped to catch as my steady. And that was all I knew about either character. So I began to give her the life I thought she should have. I decided she was an only child. She was loved and adored and spoiled to death by her father. Her mother was stern, but loving. And then I began to think as I believed this Lisa would think. *I'm an only child. I have everything I want. But Bob is somebody very special. He's going to be a doctor and that means position and money. I'm going to get him to be my boy friend if it's the last thing I do.*

Within the thirty-minute waiting period, I felt that I had developed this girl into a real human being. I did not want to walk in there and just be a pretty little actress reading lines. I wanted this part. Getting on television would be a good credit and it could lead to much bigger things.

When I went into the room where I was to audition, I met Ted Cordey, who was at that time executive producer for *World.* He was very important to the show and also a fine director. We talked for a time and he seemed to like my response to him as a human being. He was looking for somebody with a little spark and I certainly had that. Lyle Hill, who at that time was associate producer and later producer, was there, too. Ted played the part of Bob with me (there I was again reading with the person who was judging me) and when I finished the scene he told me he wanted to see me again the following week. This time I was to read with the actor Ronnie Welch, who played the part of Bob Hughes.

By the time the next audition rolled around I had truly invented an entire life for Lisa and her family. I wore the same dress again because they seemed to like me in it and I didn't want them to forget that I was the girl in the green print $7.50 shirtwaist dress that they had liked.

They took me to a small studio with a camera. There in a

control room sat Ted Cordey and Lyle Hill and I think some of the people from Procter & Gamble.

Ronnie and I sat in chairs and pretended to be sitting in a drugstore. I was not afraid of the camera because I was too busy concentrating on my character and on doing the part well. I had made a few changes in the script which I thought would show me off better. Even then I knew to change dialogue so that it worked for me, so that it sounded right for me. I certainly knew they were not just looking for a girl who could say lines. They were looking for a quality. That's what acting is all about: to create something. The important thing is to make contact with the people you are acting out a scene with.

After the audition I was told they would get in touch with my agent when they had reached a decision. On the way home the torment began. *Are they going to realize I can do the part? Do I have the right color hair? Am I tall enough? Short enough? Oh, please, please, let me have the part.* That was probably the most painful week in my career. Waiting for both the Lisa roles. It was certainly the turning point.

A few days later I was auditioning for a musical, *Take Me Along*, with Jackie Gleason and Walter Pidgeon. The show was taken from the play, *Ah, Wilderness*, which I had done during my Playhouse days so I knew the book well. I, along with dozens of other girls, was trying out for the young girl. She was shy, awkward and funny and I knew I could do the part perfectly. I was standing backstage wringing my hands, impatiently waiting for my turn when Caroline Allen came rushing over to me and said, "You've got Lisa on *As the World Turns*. How fantastic it will be if you get the movie. Now, go out there and get this show, too." I sang five songs before they decided I was not right for the part. I guess that was another time in my life I didn't mind being turned down. I was much too excited about landing the Lisa role in *As the World Turns* to feel anything else. Getting this break would give me the first real opportunity to show the public what I could do as an actress. Now I would have a chance to put into operation all that I had learned. And if I got the movie too—as Caroline said, "How fantastic it will be. . . ."

I called my family that night to give them the good news. Mother was so excited she cried and Daddy in his usual calm, easy manner expressed his delight. Even my kid brothers, who used to think soap operas were corny, congratulated me. Later they became my biggest fans and watched the show at every opportunity.

On Saturday morning I went to audition for Max Rosenberg, the producer of *Girl of the Night*. Now, I was a very different person from the girl he saw the first time. I was the young prostitute he was looking for. When Dorothy Dill and I finished he smiled and said, "My dear, you've got the part." I squealed and sprinted around that desk and nearly broke all my teeth when I kissed him.

How I got the part was by using an experience I had when in college. There was a boy who was taking some courses at our school and all the girls were after him. I decided I would get him by hating him. We played tennis one day and I got him so mad he socked me in the eye with a ball. I pretended to faint and he picked me up and carried me to the infirmary. We fell madly in love. His father was a preacher, too, so the next day, being Sunday, I decided to be the most provocative female that church had ever seen. Since my love was in the choir, I marched into that church and took a seat on the front row dressed in an outfit I had seen worn in a sexy French movie. I had on a tight black skirt, red jacket, black tam, gold gypsy earrings, my black eye was touched up with black mascara, and draped about my shoulders I wore a long fringe stole. When my love saw me, he nearly fell out of the loft. He was mine forever. So, I dressed up like that when I auditioned for the lead in *Girl of the Night*. And the part was mine.

The following week I had my first show to do on *World*. I was extremely nervous but I kept a cool façade and tried to act as though this was just an ordinary experience. As I entered the CBS lobby a guard sitting at a desk said, "Can I help you?" I very haughtily said, "I hope you can. I am Eileen Fulton." As though that was supposed to tell him everything he needed to know. He said, "Yeah?" "Well, I'm with *As the World Turns*."

Going back to his newspaper he aimed an arm. "You go to the right and walk down to the end of the hall and up the stairs." Okay, so CBS hadn't given him my name in capital letters.

I entered a small rehearsal hall with a long table in the middle and chairs all around. I was early and the room was deserted. Rehearsal started at two thirty and it was just a little after two when I arrived. I walked over to the windows and looked out on a row of brownstone houses, each with a lovely garden. I saw a man sitting on his terrace, drinking coffee and reading. It was the first warm spring day and I looked at him and thought, *How can you sit there so calmly when I'm about to die?* I was clutched with the fear that they might decide to fire me before they gave me a chance to show what I knew I was really capable of doing.

Suddenly the door opened and all these people I had been watching on television came bouncing into the room laughing, having fun and telling funny experiences, and I looked at these people and felt like my jaws had turned to stone. There were Helen Wagner, Don McLaughlin, Ronnie Welch, Santos Ortega and I can't remember how many others. Everybody was very sweet and nice to me and I have found out since that other actors like to be on our show because the actors of *World* are very gracious to newcomers, whereas I understand on some other shows they are not, they're cliquish.

Everybody sat down at the table and leafed through their scripts talking all the while about other things. I knew my script by heart. It was the same scene I had auditioned with, but I sat there, afraid to look at all these casual, happy people, and kept my eyes glued to the script. Ted Cordey entered and the room grew silent. Ted was sort of the Sandy Meisner of daytime television. When he walked in, God walked in. The Great White Father, as he was often called, had entered. He sat at the head of the table and everyone remained quiet in great reverence as though "Daddy is about to say grace."

Ted had pleasant things to say, kind and sometimes funny things, but it all went over my head because I was so terrified with the reading. Readings have always terrified me much more than the performance because once the acting has begun I become the character and I totally forget myself. At that moment,

I felt as though I was the only person who had ever had a first day with a national television show. Ted knew the other people. He knew what their capacity was. He knew they understood the characters they were playing, but I was new to him. I had never done a soap opera before and I was so afraid during the reading that afternoon that he would think, *Well, I hired her and if I don't like her today I'll fire her.*

When I learned that Helen Wagner, who plays Nancy, Bob's mother, was married to Robert Willey, a producer for whom I had auditioned the summer I graduated from the Playhouse I felt the vibrations were right for me and my fear lessened. I loved Helen immediately. She was very understanding and tried to ease my tension. She told me about her house in the country and her garden and I realized she was not just an actress but a warm, wonderful human being whose interests were very much centered on her husband and her home. Later on I learned that all of the cast were family people. I couldn't get over that they went to church, that they were doing things in their community, that they were active in so many things outside of their jobs. At that time I couldn't imagine how they could think of doing anything other than their work at the studio.

Ted took out a stop watch, pushed the button and pointed at the person who was to open the first act saying, "Cue!" The lines are paced down to the second. When my turn came, which was the last act, I talked with ease (or so I thought) and did it naturally but without animation, and Ted was wondering why I was not performing. None of the others were either, but since I was new I guess he expected me to really act out my part. My timing was off and he stopped me on every line and gave me a line reading. He wouldn't stop the other people because he knew they would come up with a marvelous performance the next day, but he didn't know what to expect from me. By the end of the rehearsal that afternoon I was very frightened of the live show I was to give at one thirty the following day. From my training at the Playhouse I had been taught to approach a role carefully, slowly, so this was something I had to learn to work with because television is a fast study.

The next morning on the way to the studio waves of nausea

flooded over me and my legs seemed made of lead. My emotions swung from absolute fear to absolute happiness. It was sort of like the feelings I had on my wedding day. Little did I know that day I would be spending many more years with *World* than I spent with Bill.

My first scene took place in a drugstore called the Sweet Shop. This was a very important meeting place on *World*, where Penny and Jeff and Ellen and whomever she happened to be in love with, would get together, so Bob and Lisa met there, too. The scene opened with me sipping a soda and talking to Bob Hughes. By the time the scene began I was completely undone. From out of nowhere organ music swelled in the air and threw me. It was completely unreal to have organ music coming in over your talking. Where was it coming from? There I sat thinking, *I am in the Sweet Shop and I am here with Bob, the boy I want to go steady with*—when suddenly I heard an organ. How could I know, since nobody bothered to tell me to expect it, that it was the theme music for the show? I hadn't noticed any music when I watched the show at home. I was completely rattled, but that was only the beginning. The soda was old, rotten milk with whipped cream squirted on top. I sat there, through the whole scene, sipping this slop, and acted like it was the greatest drink on earth. They hadn't counted on my swallowing the stuff and they nearly died because in those days they didn't use real food or drinks. Another thing that upset me terribly was the sounds of people eating. I heard knives and forks and dishes and I was furious that the cast or crew showed so little respect.

After the scene they asked me why I drank the soda. I guess they thought I was just a dumb young actress, but I said, "That's the way I am. You can't fool an audience. They know." Which I believed then to be true and certainly believe it now. It was my turn to ask a few questions and my temper was boiling. "How could you allow people to eat when I'm acting? And whoever got the idea to put organ music in a drugstore?" They thought that was pretty funny. It was. They stopped laughing long enough to explain the eating sounds were just that—sound effects. Nobody had bothered to tell me that the Sweet Shop served food. Then they told me the music was *World's* theme song.

But I was in for one more shock. I was sitting in the make-up room trying to get my legs to stop shaking after displaying my artistic temperament when Don McLaughlin, who plays Bob's father said to me, "My dear, I saw your scene and thought you were wonderful, but don't go out and buy your Rolls Royce yet, because if you have what they want to work with, you've got a job, but if you don't, it doesn't mean you aren't good because I think you are and I want you to know that. But if they don't hire you, it simply means you are not the type they are looking for." I thought that was a wonderful thing to say to me and I appreciated it, but what Don didn't know was that I didn't know the part was not mine. Irna Phillips, the show's creator and writer, who had the final say as to whether the role was mine or not would decide after she saw the show. I am so grateful I didn't know I was being auditioned in that performance because I probably wouldn't be Lisa today. There's nothing worse than having to prove yourself and had I known the truth I would have been scared out of my mind. Certainly I wouldn't have been so fresh about the sound effects and everything. But perhaps that was part of what they liked about me that day. I took my work seriously and they realized it. Before I left, I was told they would reach a decision within the next three weeks.

I walked out of there determined that if I got the role of Lisa I would make something out of that goody-goody because changing her into a character with more depth would also help me to change myself. I wanted desperately to develop *me* into something other than a carbon copy of what others wanted me to be. I was not Puritan Pearl, yet stomping around in jeans wasn't what I was after either. That was just being a bad kid. It wasn't the answer to the real me.

A week later Caroline Allen called me to say that I really, really did have the part. A contract was waiting for my signature.

A week after getting *World* I signed my contract for the movie *Girl of the Night*. There couldn't possibly have been two happier Lisas in the world than me. Caroline had promised there would be no problem with the two work schedules. *Girl* would be worked into my daytime show without conflict. How I would manage to learn the movie script plus the World scripts didn't even enter my mind. I had what I wanted and I guess I knew everything would work out. The movie was not scheduled to begin shooting for several weeks, which gave me the time to get World's Lisa on solid ground.

Once again I called my parents to tell them of my gold strike. When I told them I would be playing the part of a call girl whose name was Lisa, too, I must admit I held my breath for a few seconds, waiting for their reaction. I was greatly relieved to hear they were delighted for me. They asked after Ginger and I told them she was a joy but I was worried about leaving her alone so much. She was an angel and so very smart, but no living thing can live long without attention and affection.

At two-thirty every afternoon the following day's script of World is read for the first time and rehearsed for timing. The actual rehearsal does not begin until the next morning and by that time you have memorized your part and familiarized yourself with the dialogue of the people you will be doing a scene with.

I had only been on the show twice and Ted was still concerned about the way I gave a cold reading because my timing was off and he would inform me of this fact. He would also stop me on virtually every line and give me a line reading. At my third afternoon rehearsal I blew up and slammed my fist down on the table and said, "Damn it, don't give me a line reading. Who are you to give a line reading? You would say a line one way because you are a certain person. I could never say it your way because I am a different person. Tell me what you *want* but don't tell me how to say it!" And he looked at me with raised eyebrows over the tiny glasses he wore on the end of his nose and he just stared at me. Everybody gasped and looked down at their scripts, embarrassed. A few of the men laughed because they liked the spitfire in me. It took me a long time to learn how to talk with this man and it took me a long time to control myself and to realize he was probably as nervous about hiring me as I was about being hired. I knew he could fire me at any moment, yet I felt if he understood how I functioned as an actress we would have no more problems, because I truly liked and respected him, but he had to understand how I worked best. When he began to see what I could do with the part he became my greatest ally. Ted was responsible for my being given the opportunity to develop Lisa as I wanted her to become.

When I was rebelling against Ted I once again hopped into my jeans, sneakers and an old shirt of Bill's under the impression I would look tough so people would not push me around, but I guess all I looked was poor.

In the beginning, I would appear at the studio promptly at seven thirty to begin the rehearsal for that day's show. Actually, you don't have to be there that early unless you are in the first act. The last act is rehearsed at nine and if you happen to be in that act then you do not have to be at the studio until that time, but I was very conscientious in those days and, in fact, got there before seven thirty. I don't do that anymore because it's foolish to come in and sit around when you could be sleeping an extra hour or so, but for the first two years on the show I always came in at that time.

One thing that bothered me terribly in a TV series of this kind was that you might do only one or two shows a week and if one show was not quite up to par, you might be off television for the rest of your life. Even the greatest actor in the world can have an off day, but if you're on television and the show is live and you're new and you have one of those unexplainable off days—good-bye. Until I learned not to worry about it, it stood in my way. I remember getting notes before air from Ted telling me this was wrong and that was wrong and he would say, "You've got to play this part up more. You're not saying it with meaning!" And I would start crying and scream, "I will not *mean* what I'm saying until air. I've got so many other things to think about. I've got to get the technicalities out of the way so I can play it as it should be played. So I can be *real!*" And poor June Gossit, our make-up lady, would have to start making up my eyes all over again because I would cry off all the mascara and Ted would keep worrying me with his notes and I would keep crying and poor June would keep patching my make-up until, red-eyed, I would go on the screen and somehow it would come off pretty well.

Maybe Ted felt he had to get me charged up to do a good show because so many of the young people there, who were not regulars on the show, needed a superficial jolt to get their adrenalin going. I didn't need this. My adrenalin flows without this. Besides, I had no intention of letting college-girl Lisa disappear into the dust. She would become very much a regular on the show. If Ted would only be patient with me and give me the chance to prove myself he would see how well I performed for the live show. I am not the only person on the show who works this way, holding back until the actual performance, but back then, in the beginning, Ted was not sure of me and my skill.

During the first rehearsal in the morning we work in a room with small tables and chairs and move these around to set up our positions and gauge the approximate space we will have in a particular scene. Every line has to be memorized and we have to move on a certain line or a certain word because these are specific cues for the camera to come in on; therefore you have to be extremely exact in your delivery and timing. At nine thirty until ten twenty we have our first blocking. The sets are up and the props are on the set. Every moment and every bit of dialogue are perfected at this time. For instance, if I have a scene where I must set the dining room table, all of that is acted out because everything must be done on cue and you have to be very careful not to say a certain line facing in the wrong way or you might force the camera to shoot out into the studio, which could ruin the scene. You have to get used to the props you are working with because until you are familiar with all the technicalities, you can't concentrate on your part. For instance, if you are to make a salad, well, it isn't hard to pretend to chop up celery and lettuce, but when you actually have to work with the things in your hand you will discover the chopping takes more time than when you were pretending, so you have to work with these things all morning because walking to the refrigerator and back to the table to begin making the salad are all separate camera cuts and they must be timed to the fraction of a second. The audience is not aware how difficult these things are, because by the time you go on air, you have practiced your movements and dialogue over and over again.

In the first few weeks of being on the show I could not get over the noise on the sets when we were rehearsing. In the beginning I could not distinguish what noise was necessary, like building noise which has to be done, and what was unnecessary, like talking and walking back and forth. I have always insisted on peace and quiet when I'm rehearsing. I cannot concentrate and neither can Helen if there's a lot of commotion or talking going on around us. So I would scream and yell about this and I became a little shrew on the set. I was very difficult, but people were gradually told by John Conboy, our stage manager, to keep as quiet as they possibly could while I was rehearsing. The noise and the racket really drove me crazy until I learned not to listen. John is now the producer of *Love Is a Many Splendored Thing*. He was absolutely the most fantastic stage manager in the world. He really understood me. He was also the one who kept me from going to pieces when Ted would get me so upset, giving me notes just before air asking me to do things that I thought were impossible to play. I didn't know how to trust myself to just let go and do it. I would be very upset, crying, and June would patiently repair my tear-stained face while I screamed, "I will not do it!" And John would grin and pull up his shoulder. "Go on, get it out now. Hit me." And I would punch his arm a few times and then go on the show. Gradually, I discovered Ted was trying to help me. He saw my capabilities far better than I did at that time.

Then, at ten fifteen we have a fifteen-minute break. From ten thirty until eleven fifteen we have a run-through and try to do the show without stopping. By then the lighting should be right so there are no shadows on the set and the show at that time is pretty much the way it is supposed to be.

Eleven fifteen is our big break. We have an hour. Some people eat lunch, like Helen, who brings all sorts of beautiful organically grown vegetables from her garden. I usually wait until after the show to grab a bite.

Make-up and hair are done during that hour and we get our notes at that time as to what the director wants us to play up or down or whatever complaint or suggestion is given. At twelve twenty we have the dress rehearsal and that runs exactly half an hour with the commercials. Everything is done except the music. If it should run over or under thirty seconds or whatever, we then figure out how to pick up certain things or stretch certain things.

Sometimes, not often, something will go wrong with the timing when we are doing the live show which goes on at one thirty, and whoever has the last bit of dialogue is given a speed-up or a slow-down signal. That happened to me once and I all but fainted on the spot. I was doing a scene with Don Hastings, who was my husband, Bob (Ronnie was replaced a few months after I became his TV wife), and I was living the part, it was a real moment for me, it was really happening when suddenly out of the corner of my eye I saw the stage manager flagging his arm in a circular motion, indicating I should talk faster because we were about to go off the air, and it completely destroyed me. Suddenly I forgot the character and became Eileen out there in front of some crazy-looking cameras in front of millions of people. I panicked. I went completely berserk and I just looked at Don Hastings. "Well, you know how I feel about it and that's all I have to say. If you have something to say—say it." He looked at me and just calmly took over. He understood. I threw it in his lap very ungraciously. So he fed my line in and ended it, but after the show I screamed and ran to the producer's office where Ted and Lyle were and I came babbling in and they didn't know what I was saying so when Ted got me calmed down he looked at me like the Great White Father he is and said, "They should know better than to do that." And it never happened again. It would not have happened that time had John Conboy still been with us. The new stage manager was told if my scene had to be speeded up to give it to Don when my back was turned and let him take care of it because Don isn't thrown by anything.

As I said, our show is live every day. The only part that is taped are the baby scenes. If someone has a scene to do with a child then that scene is taped at twelve and is fitted right into the live show.

Getting accustomed to working on the sets was something else I found difficult. Each set generally has three sides, depending on how the scene is to be shot, and the fourth wall is of course where the cameras are. And while you are acting there is constant movement going on. A camera can sometimes be as close to you as three feet. The boom, which is sort of a three-wheeled ladder, has the microphone on it and this follows you around, but when these things move, they make a lot of noise and this can be distracting until you get used to it.

Years ago, before television became as perfected as it is today, we had a lot of trouble with rain scenes. Back then, the rain machines just shot rain. They couldn't be regulated. One time I had a scene with Lisa's landlady and we were standing in the kitchen, in front of the window which in those days didn't have glass, and suddenly the rain came down and in. It poured all over us. The curtains were wet, our hair was wet, water was running off our faces. No one on television could see it, but we didn't know it while the scene was taking place. Today, with the highly sensitive equipment that is used the viewer would have seen every single drop of rain.

When script rehearsals began on the movie, *Girl of the Night*, every morning I was scheduled to be at Warner Brothers, a long, sleek limousine would pick me up and out I would slouch in jeans and sneakers. I guess my doorman thought I had turned hooker. I would act like a limousine picked me up all the time, plop down in the back seat and sprawl out as though very bored. I wasn't. It was my way of acting like "the star."

One day the limousine picked me up at CBS to shoot an outdoor scene for the movie and I was in my jeans, as usual, and really moved like a hippie because I was exhausted. The scene I was to do was without dialogue. I was merely to get out of a car and walk into a brownstone building. The location shot was in the Sixties on the East Side. The lady who owned the brownstone had turned it over to us. When I got there, it was the crew's dinner break. I was very tired and I went in the make-up room and collapsed onto a bed and fell fast asleep.

When the make-up man came in and found me he thought I was some poor little kid from the country trying to make a big break in the big city.

During the next two weeks, he was so kind to me. When he made me up he was so gentle, so sweet and I couldn't quite figure him out. He was very kind and fatherly. I thought it very dear of him. I didn't know why he put himself out so much for me, but the night I did my first acting piece with John Kerr I found out.

When we finished the scene everybody applauded. They were all excited and told me how great I played it. That evening, just before I was due back for another scene, the make-up man called and said, "For the past two weeks I have been feeling sorry for you. You looked so pitiful the first time I saw you asleep on the bed and I wanted to protect you and send you back home to your parents, but when I saw you in that scene you were brilliant. You didn't deserve any of my sympathy—just my adoration."

That night, I got into character for the role. I was dolled up like a swinging hooker. The scene was to take place on the street and all the lights were on. The street looked like a block party was about to begin and people were stacked up along the curbs to watch the movie being filmed.

I was in the house, waiting for my cue when the stage manager came up to me and said, "Eileen, do you know a Bill?" I didn't think it was *my* Bill because he was in California. "I don't know." "Well, he's standing out there and he said you are his ex-wife." The stage manager laughed, "You couldn't have been married. You're too young." "Oh, I've been married." We went out and Bill was standing there, leaning on his umbrella.

"Maggie, I knew you would make it. I always knew when we were married you would make it and I wouldn't. . . ." "Bill, I . . ." It was an embarrassing moment and people were watching us. He continued as though I hadn't said a word. ". . . and I would be standing in a crowd watching you with everybody else and say, 'Isn't she great?'" He paused and studied the girl before him, who hardly resembled Maggie. Also I had dyed my hair black for the part and in the getup I had on, there wasn't a trace of Margaret McLarty.

He told me he had been traveling around the country not sure just what he wanted to do with his life. By accident, he said he walked by and asked one of the crew who was starring in the movie and when he heard my name, he couldn't resist asking for me. That meeting shook me up because our divorce was still not final and from the way he looked at me, it appeared he was interested in me again.

A few nights later I was having a bad time sleeping. I felt tense, worried and I didn't know what was bothering me, but whatever it was, it would give me no peace. I got up and went in the living room and stretched out on the sofa. I fell asleep but woke up suddenly, raced to the window, pulled up the shade. I didn't know what I was looking for, but impulse drove me. There stood Bill on the sidewalk, looking up at me. It terrified us both and he called me soon after and apologized. He said he had been in the neighborhood and happened to walk past the building and was just looking up, remembering our days together, when I appeared at the window. That episode didn't make any sense either.

The following night I had a date with a well-known bachelor who must remain nameless, and as we were coming home, I told him, for whatever reason, about seeing Bill at my window and just as we got to my building, I saw Bill standing on the corner. It might have been another coincidence, but I decided to move as soon as I could because I was not going to start dating Bill again. That divorce would go through and I would keep my distance from him.

As I was so busy, poor Gin, my dog, was left alone all the time. It was a terrible life for her but she adored me so I didn't have the heart to send her home. Yet as much as I loved her, I realized she couldn't stay with me. She was wonderful company and would sit curled up in my lap every night while I studied my scripts.

She was a very sexy dog. Even girl dogs chased her. One morning a big collie who was off his leash tried to romance her and she howled and jumped all the way up onto my head. She kept whimpering and I couldn't get her out of my hair. I saw a doctor's office and ran in to get away from the dog and to ask them to help me get her out of my hair. They looked at me like everybody in New York had a dog on their head. The nurse said, "You can't bring a dog in here." "Please let me stay until that big collie out there goes away." "No." Then I asked if I could borrow a dollar to get a cab so I could cross the street to my apartment without that dog following us. She gave me the money to get me out of the office. I tried pulling Ginger down, but her nails would stick me so I had to keep her on my head until I got home.

When I was at home, I talked on the phone a lot and she associated me with the phone. From time to time I would find the phone off the hook when I would come in. And one evening a friend called and said, "Eileen, are you all right?" She sounded so alarmed. "Why? I'm fine." "But when I called you this afternoon, you screamed and screamed and the receiver fell and you didn't pick up. The line has been busy all day." Suddenly I put two and two together. It was Ginger. That poor animal was trying to communicate with me and since she associated the phone with me, I guess she thought I was on the other end. That was her way of saying, *Please come home. Please don't leave me alone.* I explained to my friend that it was Gin who answered the phone, not me.

Ginger was afraid of big dogs and big men. One night when I came home with a tall, handsome date, the doorman (my protector) who was also the elevator man, took us up and he gave me the "thumbs down" sign on my date. He didn't like the man. I don't know how he knew the Adonis was a maniac, but his antenna was working. I grinned, thinking my doorman wrong.

When I came in, Gin took one look at this blond, blue-eyed giant and tucked her tail in, growling with jealousy and hid under a chair. I offered him a cup of tea and he offered me his body. Before I could sit down, he had me down on the couch. I gave him a hard shove and got to my feet. "I'm not that kind of girl." Then he tried to throw me on the floor. I got so mad I grabbed him by the collar and twisted his tie, pushed my elbow in his stomach and kicked his legs out from under him. My brave Ginger came out of hiding and licked him. This sex nut tried to grab me and I started screaming. "You leave me alone. Don't you dare come near me, and get out of here right this instant." My hero, the doorman, opened the door with the passkey and ordered, "Out!" I guess he had been listening all along. I truly appreciated my guardian angel of a doorman that night.

Gin was pregnant, but I didn't know it at first. I thought she was just letting herself go the way some women do. But she kept getting fat and I began to wonder about the luck of that male dog Mother had told me about. I took her to an animal hospital and the doctor told me she was pregnant. And due. My timing was perfect. Another couple of days and I would have come home to find a house full of puppies—or a dead dog.

The afternoon the pups were to arrive, I couldn't get off the set (I was shooting *Girl of the Night*) to call the hospital. But when I did call, they just said I could pick her up the next day. I did and I asked about the puppies, but no one seemed to know anything. I couldn't get anyone to tell me what had happened. Gin was all right and that was the most important thing, but I never did learn what they did to her or what happened to her babies.

I called my parents and told them they would have to take her back. I just couldn't spend enough time with her. And I told them about the pregnancy. Mother could not believe that a six-month-old dog could get pregnant.

About a week later, I sent her home by train. I felt like a beast and from that sad look, she knew. I wanted to send her by plane but my family lived in Concord, North Carolina, at that time and there wasn't an airport near enough to send her to and have Daddy pick her up. Gin is still with them and when I go home, she reminds me that she has never forgiven me for sending her away.

I remember one time, years later, Mother called to tell me that while she was watching *World* and I was in the middle of a fight scene with my TV husband, Ginger started shrieking and hid under a chair until the show was over. Mother asked me if Gin had ever witnessed anyone fighting with me. I thought it was absolutely incredible that Gin remembered the sex-mad Adonis because when I looked over my old script, there were the exact same words: "You leave me alone. Don't you dare come near me. . . ." So I told Mother about the incident.

I had now been on the show about two months and had begun to make that sweet college girl a bit conniving. Every time I found the chance to hint at marriage to Bob, I really made use of it and I approached the marriage as something *I* really wanted and I projected that. Ted Cordey by then saw what I was after. He saw my drive, my ambition as an actress and he helped me find places to put it to use within a scene.

Lisa was meant to be a temporary character, but I knew she could really add spice to the show over a long period. I took advantage of the slightest opportunity to build her character and, finally, my big chance came. Irna Phillips, the writer, had caught on to what I was up to and she liked the idea of this cunning, shrewd Lisa. The first scene showing this part of Lisa came when Bob caught the kissing sickness—mononucleosis—and Lisa came to visit, looking a little sexy, and mothered him just the way Nancy, his mother would when he was sick, and the plot was on.

The original Lisa dreamed of marrying the man she loved, living in a sweet little house with a little fence covered with climbing roses and children to take care of. The Lisa I was now allowed to show wanted to marry Bob because he was going to be a doctor, which meant a beautiful home, her own car, money and position.

As soon as Bob recovered she invited him to visit her home when her parents were away for the weekend. There was a scene with them on the couch. Lisa had talked Bob into asking her to marry him and they went into a mad embrace and kissed passionately. (We got a registered letter from California saying, "That girl should be fired! She kisses with her mouth open.") Soon after that Lisa and Bob went to the justice of the peace and the knot was tied. But the marriage was to be kept a secret since Bob was in medical school and she was in college.

When she became pregnant she had to move out of the dorm and it was at that point she went to Nancy and told her they were married and that she was going to have a baby. Well, that was a funny show. Ronnie Welch had been replaced by Don Hastings because Ronnie just didn't look old enough to be a father and Don's first day on the show as the new Bob took place when I told Nancy everything and was then to meet Bob to tell him his parents knew of our marriage. Suddenly the audience saw a new Bob. It was doubly funny because Don was known to millions over the years on other daytime serials such as *Edge of*

Night. And the next time they saw him he was playing Bob Hughes.

When Lisa moved into the Hughes' home, it was then that she began to become a real bitch and Irna developed this character brilliantly.

Being given the chance to play Lisa as I wanted to was a great experience. By then, I knew she was no longer a temporary character. But had it not been for Ted's help, it well might never have happened for me.

Some months later, and just before my movie, *Girl of the Night,* was to premiere at the Criterion Theater, I got a call to audition for a television commercial. It was for a popular beverage which I cannot name and I was to say something to my TV mother about inviting people over for dinner. Then I was to open the refrigerator, take out a soft drink and drink. I did. It was hot and it spewed and foamed all over me. They yelled, "Cut! Miss Fulton, for God's sake, girl, don't drink it, just act it." I said, "I will not indicate drinking. If I am to drink—I drink!" The voice was getting madder. "For God's sake, can't you fake it?" "How am I going to fake drinking if I hold it up and start swallowing? I can't fake it." "We said fake it and that's what we mean."

"Mother" had been furiously mixing a bowl of whateverthehell it was and when I started to do the scene over she said, "Do you suppose the little *actress* can do it this time?" I wanted to take that bowl and dump it on her head. I tried the scene again and it went all over my face again so they had to make me up again. They now agreed that I might drink and got a cold bottle. I did and the take was good. Now I was to go on to the next part of the commercial.

I started my next bit and they said, "Cut! Miss Fulton, don't play her like that. You're playing her like a teen-ager. Make her older." The four men from the advertising agency were all playing director so five men were telling me what to do and each had his own idea. I made her older, I made her younger, I made her like Katharine Hepburn, I made her like me, I made her from the North, I made her from the West, I made her from the East and they said, "For God's sake, girl, you can't even talk. You don't even have an accent. If we could only identify you with some part of the country maybe you would be believable." Then I really got nervous and couldn't do anything because they didn't know what they wanted and the woman I played the scene with kept looking at me and stirring that damn bowl and making tisking sounds and staring at me in exasperation. I could have killed her.

Suddenly they put all the lights on me. I felt like an insect being studied through a microscope, and a voice bellowed over the speaker, "Eileen Fultonnnn, listen to this tape." I did. It was the one that I choked on because the drink was hot. "Thattt issss terrible!" Everybody was standing around, all these extras, waiting for the next scene and staring at me like, Look at the bad actress. Finally, I had had it and I yelled out, "You don't know what the hell you want!" And hell was a very strong word for me to use at that time so it came out like ——you! I put a lot of power into it and it so shocked them they didn't say a word for at least sixty seconds. "You want it like this and you want it like that and you don't know at all what you really want and you think I don't have an accent? Weyall honey, ah got one!" "Quiet her down, take her out, take her to dinner, get her out of here."

They took me to dinner and I ordered everything. I ordered squab (I didn't know at that time squab was a pigeon), but I was so mad I couldn't take the first bite of anything so I sat there and stared at those four goons. They were all laughing and talking and one said, "You know, we're going to have to let you go. Where did you learn to act?" I said, "Well, if you want to watch, I'm on *As the World Turns* every day and I've got a movie opening tomorrow night and I happen to have the lead! I'll send you a pass." I leaned forward and really gave them what for. "I've never seen such a group of idiots in my life. Nobody knows what they want and you blame it on me!"

Their accounting department made a beautiful mistake and I got paid for the commercial for a year and a half! I collected over two thousand dollars in residuals for it. There's justice. I kept the money because I deserved it. There was a double indemnity to it. That woman who played my mother was an extra on *World* years later. I never forgot her so when I saw her one day in the hall at CBS, I knew who she was instantly. She came up to me and said, not recognizing me, "Where is my dressing room?" My peacock feathers were showing, "Well, the stars' rooms are down here. The extras go down the hall." That gave me such pleasure, because she was an extra. With an attitude like hers, no wonder. You can't be big unless you think big. And when you're big, you don't think about people being "little."

In November the movie opened. Mother and Charles came up and Ronnie Welch, my ex-Bob, was my escort. The opening took place at 2:00 A.M. They thought it the right time for such a film. They had all these phones outside the theater and when you picked up a receiver a sexy voice said, "Hello, why don't you come up and see me in *Girl of the Night*."

The thing Warner Brothers overlooked was that the theater was being renovated. To get in, you had to walk on planks and step over lumber. Barrels of cement were all over the lobby. Some big opening. Derelicts who had no place else to sleep were in the theater. Every bum in New York I think came to my opening. I was very crab conscious since my experience with Bill so I carried a can of spray and sprayed off all our seats. The movie was two hours' long and it was very dull. We then had a party at Reuben's with the producer, a few of his friends, my friends and family. We had sandwiches, talked for a while and that was it. I had to be up at five thirty so I had thirty minutes' sleep that night.

I dragged myself through a tough day at the studio and waited for the reviews. Most of the reviews were terrible but *Variety* said, "Watch out for this kid—she's great." My morale got to its feet and managed to get me through the rest of the day.

A few days after *Girl of the Night's* premiere, I was on the set during a *World* rehearsal and John Conboy said, "Eileen, you need to buy some clothes." "But I've got two dresses." He had on his earphones so he was listening to the director at the same time, but he was fascinated by my remark. He could not believe that I thought two dresses were all I needed. I did. "Eileen, you keep that dress on a wire hanger. I can see the marks." Well? So what?

Did it matter? "But John, this is a nice dress that I can dress up or down." I wore it with beads to dress it up and a chain to dress it down. What was wrong with that? "What do you do with all your money?" "I save it. I invest it." "How much do you spend a month on food?" "Thirty dollars." "Thirty dollars for an entire month?" I thought he thought that was a lot. "Well, I had an extra steak and I had company once this month." He couldn't believe I was real. "I spend thirty dollars in a *week* on food!" I was very surprised to see he thought me a Scrooge. The director was getting furious because John was so busy with me he wasn't giving me my cues. "Do yourself a favor, Eileen, and buy some clothes."

At that time, I knew I lacked something, but I really didn't know how to look smart. I wanted to buy clothes, but I didn't know where to begin so, with John's advice firmly fixed in my mind, I headed for the nearest department store, bought four dresses, shoes and bags to match and went home and threw up. Spending money scared me to death and the dresses had no particular style. I bought them for their colors.

When I would go for auditions I would look at other girls and admire the way they were put together. When I would see a professional model I would make notes of what she wore and how the effect looked. It never occurred to me to study fashion magazines. I just didn't identify with high fashion. I was an actress. Fashion, to me, wasn't necessary, yet I wanted to be pretty and I didn't know where to begin.

Right after I started to buy clothes, my feet started to bother me. I bought shoes to match not to fit, and my feet started to cramp all the time. I went to a doctor about my feet and she suggested I have my shoes made. My immediate reaction was, "They cost too much." And once again I heard, "Well, who are you working for? You've got money." I wouldn't listen and my feet really got in bad shape. I finally had to wear old ladies' shoes with a special arch. The cost of my embarrassment was far more expensive than if I had taken the doctor's advice from the beginning.

Summertime was even worse. There I was, in cute cotton

dresses and these black lace-up shoes with stack heels. They made me feel so homely. When I would have appointments I'd take a pair of my dainty high heels in a paper bag and when I would get to my appointment I would put on my heels so I would look pretty and then, after the interview I would stand outside the office door and get into those clodhoppers again.

I'll never forget one warm and lovely afternoon I was clumping down the street, wearing a pink fluffy dress, and a couple of guys spotted me and were all puckered up for a whistle when they got down to my feet and the whistle just froze on their lips. That upset me terribly and as I walked along, feeling very sorry for myself I stepped in a hole, and the hole kept following me. Then I looked down to see why there were so many holes on that side of the street only to discover I had lost my heel way back there where the boys had been standing. I hobbled back after it, took off my shoes, and walked down Broadway barefoot. My feet felt much better and so did I and when people looked at me they just thought I was cracked which was better than thinking I was an old lady with a face job.

That fall I caught onto the suit look. Suits were safer than dresses when you didn't know anymore than I did about what to wear. So one day, I had on this smart-looking black suit and I wore it to an audition. My agent had arranged for me to read for a very famous director-producer and when I walked in, feeling quite neatly groomed he growled, "Arrhh, no. If you want to be in the movies you gotta wear it low cut. You gotta wear it showing off your bust. Showing off your fanny, showing off, showing off. Come over here and let me see what you look like." He had his arms out. "Good-bye. If you want to see me showing off what I've got, go see me in my movie, *Girl of the Night.* I'll send you a pass." I didn't wait to get outside his office door to put on my monster shoes. I did it right there and made as much noise going out as I could. My respect for that great man was dumped in the nearest litter basket.

By that time my blue jeans rebellion had ended, but my search for self was still my preoccupation. And something happened on a visit home that summer to boost my confidence so much that I made a big breakthrough and the credit was all Lisa's. The girl *I* created.

The experience was also mystifying because it was identical to a dream I had had as a little girl. The day I arrived I found dozens and dozens of women crowded around the house and standing out in the yard, looking at me expectantly. I thought they were members of Daddy's congregation. Or perhaps Mother was having a luncheon or something. But when I came up the walk they all started flocking around me. "Are you Lisa?" My peacock feathers began to show. "Yes, do come in." I still didn't realize they were there just to see me. When I got inside, nobody was home. I couldn't figure that out. Surely these women were expected.

They jammed the house all talking to me at once. They wanted to know about Bob and Chris and Nancy and they were chattering away. When my dad walked in, he thought they were friends of mine so he went to the kitchen to make coffee for them.

Mother was teaching school and when she walked in and saw the house bulging with women, she nearly fainted. She couldn't even get to me so she ran up the stairs to her bedroom to change into something more comfortable or to cry, I don't know which, and a few moments later my dad called me to the phone. New York wanted me back immediately for an important audition. I was bewildered by the people and more so by the phone call. I looked at Daddy's forlorn expression because he gathered from my conversation I was leaving. "I guess this is a hello and a good-bye. I'd better see Mother." I started moving through the crowd toward the stairs and Mother was standing at the foot, wearing a robe and looking mortally upset. I told her I had to turn right around and fly back. She shouted above the jabbering, "You will just have to excuse my daughter, please, I haven't even had a chance to see her and now she's leaving us." She wanted them to leave and she grabbed my hand and started to march me up the stairs. I said, "Aren't these people friends of yours?" "No! Are they friends of yours?" "No." Daddy came over and said, "I don't know who they are, either." He told them nicely to please leave. It was then we realized they were my fans! Lisa had established herself. That moment, for me, was a great victory.

The show I had to go back to audition for was *Fantasticks*. It's a musical comedy and is now in its eleventh year. The story is sort of the opposite to *Romeo and Juliet*. A girl and a boy who live next door to each other become the central figures in a plot to bring them together by their fathers. The fathers pretend to hate each other and build a wall separating them (the wall is invisible but the audience is made to know there is a wall) hoping this will make the youngsters fall in love and marry. They begin courting on each side of the wall. The fathers decide to rush things and have the girl, Louisa, abducted by a dashing, handsome man, knowing this will make the boy realize he loves her and go after her and, hopefully, marry her. He finds her, they marry and are soon bored with each other so they separate and each goes out to see the world. They return to their respective homes and fall in love naturally without the need of a plot and live happily ever after.

I got the part. By day I was the syrupy, conniving Lisa. And by night I was a zany, cute kid. I had to give up all my boy friends when I got *Fantasticks* because of my work schedule. My day started at CBS at 7:30 A.M. and ended every night at 11:15 P.M. Having to check them out was a horrible conflict but I made my choice. My career came first and always will.

The show was in a small theater and there was only one dressing room so I had to share it with all the boys. They put up a screen for me because I was so modest. Actually, I've learned since that people in a company aren't aware of your body. They have a show to do and that's all they see or think about. It was during costume changes that I learned to swear.

If only I had listened to my brother Jimmy when he was a baby, I could have been a master at it. Jimmy gathered his knowledge by listening to the peach farmers who parked their trucks on the street next to our house. Jimmy was only two, but he was smart. He applied what he learned and his application nearly sent Mother back to the mountains of North Carolina where she was born.

One day while doing her grocery shopping with Jimmy in her cart, he yelled, "I want some friggin' cookies!" Out of the mouth of this infant with his golden curls and rosy cheeks came pearls of mud. Mother snatched him up as all eyes watched in amazement and, leaving her cart full of groceries, she raced out, never to darken that grocery store again. I doubt that those peach trucks were ever seen parked near our house again either.

The boys in my show tried to be very careful of their language in front of me. I was Sweetie to them, but I didn't know how to tell them I wasn't a bonbon and then, by accident one night my opportunity was given to me. One of the boys somehow cracked his head on the door and he let out, "Goddamnit!" Then, seeing me, he blossomed into a rosy flush, "I'm sorry, Eileen." I said, very loudly, for all to hear, "Hell, that's all right." They loved me after that and said what they felt like saying. I kept my ears pinned back, hoping to learn lots of cuss words. Swearing made me feel free. I loved it.

I had been with the show a few months and we were getting excellent reviews when CBS read in the papers that I was in the *Fantasticks*, which they had not known. They asked if I would let the publicity department follow me around for *A Day in the Life of Eileen Fulton*, which was to be sold to a magazine. Well, I really felt like a star, I was thrilled.

At five thirty in the morning on the appointed day, a photographer and a writer appeared at my door. I met them for real in my old housecoat, my hair just brushed back and hanging, no make-up. That was the real me in the early morning. I let them in and went about my morning routine while they took pictures and asked questions.

They looked around my tiny studio apartment and tried to find something worth using for the article. I should have had a decorator fix it up when I moved in but I didn't know what a decorator was then. I had a bed which was a bed, not a couch, and I hadn't bothered to make it up that morning since I was going to play my day realistically. I had a butterfly chair, a bucket chair, the ice-cream parlor chairs and table from Bill's and my marriage. They admired the dining table and thought it was an antique because it had so many fork holes and dents from all the fights with Bill.

I slugged down my breakfast reading my script as I ate, threw the dishes in the sink, ran in the bathroom (I did dress in private), got dressed and left without make-up while they took pictures and asked more questions.

When we got outside I started for the bus stop and the photographer told me to hail a cab. "Oh, I never take a cab. The bus gets me there just as fast." No, it wouldn't look right for the article. When they insisted I hail a cab, I felt like I was deceiving the public.

I stood there and waved, but couldn't get a cab, so I resorted to my usual method—I whistled through my teeth and about four cabs headed toward us. My whistling rather startled the two lambs.

We went to the CBS studio and the photographer took pictures all morning during rehearsals. I had the usual nerves and sat quietly in a corner going over my lines. The pictures were very interesting. I had my hair in curlers all morning.

I had lined up all kinds of appointments for the afternoon. I went to the bank, had a voice lesson and the photographer took pictures while I was vocalizing. You know, with my mouth wide open and all my fillings showing. Then I went down to the Village to be interviewed for a movie and the photographer passed out from hunger. They sent another one. I never ate, so I was accustomed to going on my own energy, but I will admit by six o'clock, I began to have a feeling of being a bit lightheaded. We all went to a restaurant there in the Village but I was too excited and I guess too tired and I couldn't eat when the food was served. I drank a glass of water. The writer felt sorry for me and bought me a bouquet of violets.

We then went to the theater as I had a show to do. When they found my dressing room was with the boys, they thought that a camp so they took loads of pictures of all of us in the dressing room. Then I said, "You can't take any more shots now. I have to be quiet for a while." They promptly vanished and I was so exhausted and thought, *Can I sing? Nothing is worth a bad performance. What have I done? My best publicity is my performance.* I really didn't think I had it in me to do the show. I was totally worn out and then the overture began and I danced out, praying I could do the show. When I looked out the only person I saw was Patsy Bruder, who plays Ellen on *World*, sitting down front with her husband and her hands were clasped like, "I can't wait!" I saw her and no one else. That sweet face was like a shot of adrenalin and I gave a good performance. It was a marvelous show, easy, and I enjoyed it. She gave me what I needed. She reminded me that your audience is all there is. Whatever you feel doesn't count when you're out there. You owe them something and whether sick or tired, you give them what they came for. I did.

Well, the photographer took pictures until the end of the curtain call. P.S. The pictures were so unglamorous they couldn't sell the story. So my bee-busy day went for nothing but it taught me an important lesson. People don't want to see a personality who looks and dresses like the girl next door.

I had been in *Fantasticks* about eight months and we had recently gotten a new stage manager. He was another "artistic murderer" like that miserable schoolteacher Mrs. Minerva I had had. He didn't like me and he didn't like Paul, the boy I played opposite in the show. This rat-fink was always giving me notes on how he wanted me to play a scene just before I would go on which would upset me terribly. He did it on purpose, obviously, and he would stand in back of the house and watch me while I was on stage and that would so frighten me I would make mistakes. So one night, I had had him up to my teeth and I said, "Who are you to give me a note before I go on? Give it to me afterward and *not* before!" He stood there and hated me with his mean eyes.

Paul was due for a vacation and the night before he was to leave somebody stole his pants and my ponytail. In the foyer of the lobby were pictures of the cast. My picture and Paul's had been turned upside down. We knew somebody in the show did not love us.

When Paul came back from his vacation he found his picture was not even in the lobby—upside down or not—it was gone.

And in his place was a picture of his roommate, who had been given his role by the stage manager while he was away. His roommate had been his stand-in and when Paul was replaced I knew I was next so I quit.

Just before I left, I took a plastic bag full of toilet cleaner and a brush to the theater thinking I'd clean out the terrible john which usually had rats in it, as a thoughtful gesture for the boys I would certainly miss. I put the brush and powder in my purse and forgot about it. On the way home that night on the subway I looked down to see white stuff all over my lap. The powder had eaten through the bag and all the way through my purse. I was out of my mind with fear. I did not have gloves and I was afraid if I got it on my hands and I began to sweat it would eat up my hands. I guess I looked like some kind of a nut sitting there wild-eyed, staring at my hands. When my stop came, I sort of held the purse in the crook of my arm without touching it with my hands and got off the train and flew into the nearest bathroom to get rid of it and save whatever I could in my purse. I had visions of my appointment book being completely devoured by those crystals, but it was intact. An appointment book is an actor's Bible. It tells you how to live, believe me. And I was to audition for a cigarette commercial the next afternoon and without that book I wouldn't know where to go or what time I was due.

I left the CBS studio at four in the afternoon the next day and hurried over to the agency to try out for the commercial. It had been a busy day at the studio and I hadn't stopped for lunch. It didn't occur to me that smoking on an empty stomach might make me sick.

When I got there they offered me a seat, gave me a cigarette, lit it and said, "May we see your right profile? Now take a long inhale." I did. "May we see your left profile?" I swung around on the chair and fell off. I looked up and tried to smile. "Honest, I know how to smoke." They looked down. "Sure you do, but this is a color commercial and you are a pale green. That will never do." We laughed, but I cried on the way home because I didn't get the commercial. They wouldn't believe it was because I hadn't eaten all day. When I thought of all the money I lost I began to view my stomach as a cash register. I started eating regularly.

Caroline Allen, at Mr. McCaffrey's, went with me a couple of days later on to an audition for a Broadway show. I can't remember the name. It was either *All American* or *Tall Story*. By now I had begun to look well turned out in clothes and when we went up to the producer's office they took one look at me and said, "I'm sorry, you're too pretty." Again I pleaded to be given a second chance. They gave me a script and Caroline and I thought of the best way to make me homely. I wore those ugly klunky shoes that laced up, an old shirt of Bill's, a long skirt, black tights and a pair of dimestore glasses. I pulled my hair back with a rubber band and I was everybody's grandmother.

We went back and I read again. The associate producer took Caroline aside and asked, "Is she your client?" "Yes." "She's marvelous but you gotta teach that kid how to dress. You gotta do something about her looks." He wasn't there the first time I read and he wouldn't believe Caroline that I had deliberately made myself up like that. They hired somebody else who was fat —and fat I couldn't be overnight.

Not long after that I went up for a musical. They were looking for actors and singers who danced. I sang, I read, I was asked to stay. Then, "Put on your dance togs." Dance togs? I just hiked up my skirt, tucked it under my panties. The choreographer gave me a few steps to try, I did all right and then I was told to do a solo run, leap and jump. I started to run and as my skirt fell it caught around my legs and I did a kind of flip and fell to the floor. "Thank you. Are you interested in comedy?" Very eagerly I said, "Oh, yes." "Well, this is a straight play." And they laughed a lot. I didn't.

The very next day I tried out for another Broadway show. The play I tried out for was *The Wall*. I was told I didn't look Jewish so I told them to please let me come back the next day and I would look Jewish.

I ran home and dyed my hair black. (It was a good thing that *World* was not in color at that time.) Bought a black braid and pinned my hair up and wrapped the braid around it, borrowed a Star of David from a Jewish friend and the next day went charging into the producer's office and was intercepted by his secretary. She would not let me go in. I couldn't be stopped for long so I ran into his office yelling, "I'm here! See? I'm Jewish!" The casting director gasped. "My God, we've just signed the girl. If only you had looked like this yesterday." So there I was, stuck with dyed black hair—

For a few weeks I was very depressed at having come so close to getting the part, but I was in the process of moving to another apartment so that took my mind off my loss. I was happy doing *World*, but as with all actors you want constantly to use your talents doing other things. I moved to a securely built old building on the West Side and the day I moved in I wore a pair of my brother's jeans and a funny sweater with hanger marks on the shoulders. The doorman asked me twice what my name was so I said, "Fulton. Like Fulton Fish Market," so I knew he would identify with that and remember my name.

Soon after I moved I went to the opening of *Cleopatra*. I had on a gorgeous black-and-white silk gown with a trumpet skirt, loads of white furs around my face, and a handsome date at my side. As we crossed the lobby floor, the doorman opened the door, his eyes bugging out at me. "You dress real good to be working in a fish market." Until that moment, I had wondered why he would never hold the door for me when I came in. After that, he all but tore the door down to let me in and out.

A few weeks later I got the part of Ann Rutledge in the play *Abe Lincoln in Illinois*, with Hal Holbrook. The day I auditioned I gave a good reading for a change and the director, Stuart Vaughn, said I was excellent. He asked if I could work it out with *World* and I told him yes. Then he said he could not give me a definite answer until he saw one other girl he was interested in. I got mad. "Why should you see another girl when you've got me?" He laughed and nodded. "You're right. You've got it." I jumped off the four-foot-high stage, ran up the aisle, hugged him, kissed him and nearly knocked him down. I did the same thing to the producer after I asked in disbelief, "Have I really got it?"

The play was for children primarily so our performances were at four o'clock every afternoon but on Friday and Saturday nights we did two shows a night for adults.

Our first dress rehearsal was done in a state of shock. Hal Holbrook was portraying Abe and when he walked out on that stage, it was like Abe Lincoln had returned from the dead. No one could act. We were spellbound. Here was the man on the penny.

It was such an emotional experience that we all cried. Hal did not get the best reviews and he should have. He spent weeks studying Lincoln. He brought the man back, even to the scratchy voice. The critics compared him to Raymond Massey's portrayal of Lincoln and talked of Massey's great rolling tones. Well, Abe didn't have rolling tones. Hal was playing the man and not just the part.

I adored Hal and he smoked big cigars so when we would be relaxing in our dressing rooms, I would sit next to Hal and do everything he did. When he'd put his feet up on the dresser and smoke, I would put my feet up and smoke little cigars which made my fillings feel like they were going to fall out. While he sipped a glass of brandy, I would sip a brandy glass full of beer. The only thing he did that I wouldn't do was take curtain calls.

During the curtain calls the *dear* little children would shoot paper clips onto the stage and I wasn't about to lose an eye over a curtain call. And one day Hal got it in the face. Those little monsters were dangerous, but we couldn't figure out where they were buying the clips and rubber bands. Then, someone in the show found out they were getting them from a candy store near the theater. Before that show closed I was probably the only person in the cast who didn't get hit. Sometimes those brats would even shoot them during a performance. I never did another children's show.

I got the part of Honey for the matinee company of *Who's Afraid of Virginia Woolf?* while doing *Lincoln*. Someone from the *Woolf* office saw me in the show and asked if I would read for the Honey role. I did and I loved the part, but my new agent didn't want me to take the part. "Eileen, I don't think this is the best vehicle for you." But it came out like, "What makes you think you can get the part?" Signing with her was a big mistake, but she had promised to make me a star and I, foolish girl, believed her in the beginning. I should have stayed with Caroline Allen and Mr. McCaffrey. Well, she certainly didn't give me the moon and the stars she promised. All she gave me was a hard time. I spent more time going to Mr. McCaffrey for advice than I spent going to her for jobs. So after her smart remark about the part of Honey I didn't bother her with further mention of it except to send her commission to her, which she certainly didn't deserve, but I had no choice—she was my agent.

My idol Alan Schneider was directing *Woolf* and when I signed to do the show he said, "Where were you when we were casting originally?" So I told him my agent had refused to submit me.

But while I was going through the waiting period before I knew I had the part I heard all sorts of gossip about someone else getting the part and I asked Alan if I had the part or not. He told me I did and to be patient. Then, a few days later a friend said somebody had been signed for it. Alan was in Washington and I called him frantically. "Do I have the part or not?" He screamed, "My God, yes. You've got it. Now will you leave me alone?" I panted my promise. I went to see my agent and told her I had the part. She said, "You're a fool. I've seen girls fall on their faces trying to play this role. What makes you think *you* won't?"

The play was not an easy one to do so they had a matinee company and I was to be the afternoon Honey. I had signed the contract without telling the producer of *World*, but I knew I had to tell him and I wanted the part so badly I just went ahead and signed, somehow thinking I would convince the producer when the time came.

What I hadn't counted on was the time of the matinee shows. The play, being longer than most, began at two instead of the usual two thirty and *World* was over at two. How could I be in two places at once? I was frantic.

Helen Wagner, my TV mother-in-law, Nancy, solved the problem for me. I was all upset, crying when I told her the show started on the dot of two and she said, "Now before you do anything rash, let's figure this out. I think I know a way."

At that time, our studio was in Grand Central Station and she told me there was a shuttle train that would take me right to the theater if I got on the front car and went out the Forty-first Street exit which was right next door to the Billy Rose Theater. She borrowed a stop watch and at two, when our show was over, she pushed the pin and yelled, "Go!" We raced for the elevator, ran down to the shuttle train, got on the front car, jumped off at

Times Square, ran up the Forty-first Street exit steps, ran all the way to the theater, shot past the backstage doorman, who must have thought we were a couple of nuts, ran all the way to the stage and looked at the watch. We did it in no time flat. It wouldn't take long to get into costume so I had no problem. Now all I had to do was talk my new producer into letting me do the show.

When I went to see him he flatly refused me. I explained that it would not interfere with World. "I still have not given my permission." He was being very unreasonable and I could not change his mind.

I called Mr. McCaffrey because he handled my World contract and I told him my predicament. "I'll make an appointment for us and assure him the play will not conflict." He did and we went to talk with the unreasonable producer. Mr. McCaffrey explained, as I had tried to do, that the two shows would not conflict. The producer smiled malevolently. "We won't let you do it." "I am going to do it!" He took my hand and gave me one of those phony sugar-coated smiles. "My dear, that will be a breach of contract." I gave him the same sugary smile. "I don't have a contract." My ace which I had discovered that morning while looking over my contract. He paled a bit. "What do you mean?" "My contract is up as of today." He turned snow white. He got out his book and said faintly, "My God, you're right. But you have to sign another contract." "I will, but you must put in writing that I can have Wednesdays off." Mr. McCaffrey sat back in amazement, appearing proud of his daughter-client.

The next day I signed the new contract and went to my first rehearsal of Woolf. I got along beautifully with the cast, but the lighting men, the people backstage, were very trying. They would make a lot of noise when I was back there preparing for a scene and I always have to have quiet when I'm concentrating, but the more I would ask them to be quiet, the noisier they became. They would play cards and shuffle them a hundred times just to drive me up the wall.

Because I had to drink so much on stage (Honey was a lush), I always had to go to the bathroom after all that tea and there's a scene where Honey exits to go to the john and Eileen really does. One of the tricks those men would pull on me was to lock the john door because they knew I always ran for it and I would have to race all the way up five flights to the bathroom. I only had a couple of minutes before I was due back on the stage so I had to take those steps two at a time.

One afternoon we had a small bonfire on stage. Elaine Stritch, who was now playing Martha, accidentally dropped her cigarette ashes down into the right end of the couch. She did not realize a bonfire was beginning or she certainly would have stuck her hand down there and put the ashes out, but after her scene she walked off and the two men who were on were at the opposite side of the stage and were not aware of what had happened. Well, the smoke started rising and the audience probably thought it was in the act. I was backstage when this happened and did not know where all the smoke was coming from. I was preparing for my next scene and the stage manager came up to me and said, "I hate to interrupt you, Eileen, but we've got a serious problem. The right end of the couch is on fire. Would you please try to cry it out when you go on?"

I went out saying, "Bells, bells, I hear bells. . . ." I'm supposed to be cracked, crazy and drunk, so I ad-libbed like mad. "I smell smoke, too. Oh, everything is going wrong. Even the sofa is burning." And I fell back on that end of the couch and sloshed my bottle of liquor all down into the side of the couch, crying all over it, and put out the fire. Then the audience realized what I had done and started applauding.

The next day the papers were full of the incident. One article said, "Eileen Fulton ad-libbed lines Edward Albee never wrote while dousing the blaze with her drinks and her tears."

Not long after that, some of the people from Procter & Gamble came to see the show. It's a good thing I did not know they were in the audience until after my performance. I would have been so nervous I might have started my own fire. Procter & Gamble have always been interested in my career and they have seen me in almost every play I've been in, which I take as a great compliment.

We had a lot of mishaps during my year with the show. One night I was slugging down my brandy (colored water) and getting stoned. But, after my first swig, I felt something grating on my teeth and right on stage I stuck my thumb under my teeth to find this "foreign particle"—only to see blood on my thumb. I ran my thumb around until I found it. Glass. I could see tiny pieces of glass in the bottom of my glass and what to do? So I started staggering around and slopping it all over everybody and they kept refilling my glass and I kept spilling it to keep from drinking it and proceeded to get drunker and drunker without taking the next swallow. I grabbed my skirt and sort of wiped the inside of the glass without making it obvious what I was doing and then I put the glass down on the bar and, somehow, stuffed my elbow into it by accident and could not get my elbow out. I had been laughing and brought my elbow drunkenly down on the bar only to land it in the glass. That was a funny scene with everybody trying to keep a straight face as they took turns tugging on the glass. The audience thought it was part of the act and since we couldn't get the glass loose, it *was* part of the act.

That same evening we were to give a performance at Hofstra University on Long Island. A limousine picked us up and the four of us were jabbering away when we noticed the car wasn't moving. Dead motor. They sent us another car and once again we all piled in. We were to meet the producer, Richard Barr, at the college and he was taking us to dinner, then back for the show. Donald Davis told the driver, "Hofstra University." The driver nodded and we settled comfortably back and once again began jabbering about anything and everything when suddenly we were at an airport. The driver says, "Here you are. La Guardia." We screamed. "La Guardia?" It was getting late and we didn't have the vaguest notion of how to get to Hofstra. The first driver had received his instructions ahead of time, but when they sent another, they forgot to tell him and this man didn't speak English too well and understood it even less.

We were lost all over Long Island, but finally about fifteen minutes after the curtain was to go up we pulled into Hofstra University. Richard Barr was standing on the sidewalk looking nervous and writing a speech. He thought we were dead so he was preparing a eulogy to all of us. There had been a terrible accident on the highway and he thought he had lost us all.

We were slapping make-up on as we hurried along the street with Mr. Barr and ran in to do the show without food or drink! That's the only performance I ever gave when I enjoyed the fake brandy.

A few days after the burning couch we had a burning building. Mine. It was evening and I was curled up in a chair studying my script for the following day's show on World when I heard the clanking of fire trucks. I went to my windows to investigate and saw all these firemen looking up at me. Smoke was pouring out of the lobby. I remembered my college training so I grabbed my favorite clothes and dumped them on the bedspread, then the lights went out and I did, too. I grabbed my script and flew out in the hall yelling, "Help me." Then I heard my phone ringing so I ran back in to answer it. It was Ted Cordey, our executive producer. He said, "I've got your cuts for tomorrow's show." "Can't talk to you now, Ted, my house is on fire. Good-bye."

I ran out in the hall again and Adolph Gottlieb, a famous painter, and his wife came out of their place to me. "Poor little thing, it's all right." His wife hugged me and guided me into their apartment and gave me a tranquilizer with a cup of tea. The fire was put out, the lights went on and they took me back to my place. I hung up all my clothes and called Ted back. "I'm awful sorry I hung up on you like that, but I thought my house was burning down." He thought that was pretty funny and the next day in Dorothy Kilgallen's column she wrote, "Recent fire in apartment house of Eileen Fulton demonstrated there's no people like show people. While paintings and furs were being licked by flames Eileen grabbed the one thing she thought important—her script, then ran."

There was yet another fire that needed putting out. I had a burning desire to do Fantasticks again so when I got a call saying the girl who was doing it was leaving and would I consider the part I said yes in capital letters. I knew they had a different stage manager so I had no fear of going back. I went right into the show as though I had never been away from it.

My first night back, the narrator for the show came over to me and said, "About a year ago I saw you on the subway acting crazy and staring at your hands." I squealed hysterically, remembering the night I had the toilet cleaner all over my lap, so when I recovered I told him about it and we both had a good laugh.

Now I was doing *World* several days a week and *Fantasticks* every night. Saturdays were rough because I did the *Woolf* matinee and then we did two shows back to back with *Fantasticks* and on Sundays we had a matinee and an evening show. Monday was dark so that was the only night I had to catch up on sleep unless I had a Monday show to do on *World*, but I was doing what I wanted and happiness is a great driving force. I never looked better in my life than in that year. Also, it was at that time that I began to work on my nightclub act. Henry Fanelli, the harpist in *Fantasticks*, and I spent an hour or so after the show working on material for the act on the evenings I did not have a show to do on *World*. Or, sometimes, we would meet early at the theater and go over my numbers.

One Sunday—it must have been a holiday—we had the day off so I called Jan Wallman, who had a showcase club called the Upstairs at the Duplex, and asked her if I could try out my act that Sunday. She said we could and so we set out for the club.

Henry was having a problem with that big harp. There were no moving trucks on Sunday so, finally, we found a friend of his who let us borrow his station wagon. We wrapped that magnificent harp in my best quilts and blankets and, with the help of another friend of his, we managed to get the harp in the wagon. We arrived at the club and found the door to the wagon locked so we had to find a locksmith. It was getting late and I was worried Jan wouldn't let me go on.

We got the harp out and started up the stairs, but we couldn't get it up. The ceiling was too low. Jan told us to try coming in through the back of the building. We got around to the back and managed to get it up the stairs but the doorway was too low so we removed part of the doorframe. Whew! At last we were in.

Jan gave me a wonderful introduction: "Dirty Lisa." Some drunk yelled, "I hate her." Everybody thought that funny so they all laughed. I held onto my cool, but I was shaking apart and when the yukking quieted down, I went into my first song and the drunk started again, "Get off the floor, dirty Lisa. Off!" I stopped singing and looked at him like an evangelist. "Ahhh, you poor thing," and held my hands out to him. He fell apart. He rolled his head around trying to focus and sighed, "I think I love her." That set the pace for the room and everybody started loving me and applauding like mad so I thought, *This is it. I've made it in nightclubs now. I'll be famous as a singer in no time.* No time is what I got for a while. Jan offered me a booking and the week I was to open, she closed.

That was a highly emotional period for me. I wanted to leave *World* because Lisa, at that time, I felt had outwitted herself. She had done all the scheming and conniving I thought she could do and I was not happy with the self-pitying creature she had become. She had fallen in love with a man named Bruce who was played by Jim Pritchett, now on *The Doctors*, and had an affair with him and left Bob for him. She told Bob she wanted a divorce and after the divorce, she lost custody of her son, Tom. Then she flew to Bruce's apartment only to find a blonde there. Then, she went back to Bob, pleaded with him to take her back, but he wouldn't. The Hughes family had lost respect for her and she was wallowing in self-pity and running back and forth, week after week, from Bob to the Hughes family, pleading with them to help her to get Bob back. I was sick of her and none too happy playing a whining role like that. I felt I was no longer giving *World* my best anymore. And I wanted to devote more time to my singing and to have the time during the day to audition for plays and musicals.

I explained to the producer the way I felt and asked if they would release me from my contract. They were very understanding and asked that I stay on for three more months. I agreed and it was settled.

Irna Phillips came to the studio one day when she learned of my leaving. She asked me why I wanted to quit and I said, "Because I feel there are other things I should be attempting. I want desperately to sing. I've got to try it." Instead of being angry as I expected, she said, "I understand. We must be honest with ourselves." And then she kissed me on the cheek. As I followed her out of my dressing room, I could read the faces of the people on the show who passed by. It was like, "Oh, brother, Eileen must have really gotten it." I did. I got understanding.

Two weeks before I left *World* I quit *Fantasticks*. I wanted to be completely free to accept something totally new and I knew *Woolf* was on a limited run and would probably close in a week or so.

My last day on the show was a sobby one. Helen Wagner came to my dressing room and we hugged and kissed and cried. Don McLaughlin spoke for the cast. He said, "We offer you our love and understanding and best wishes. Please keep in touch because we will always be interested in what you are doing." I think Don admired me for having the courage to leave a sure thing like that with nothing waiting. I now had no agent, and no manager but at that time I thought I was doing the right thing.

I remember walking out of the building and looking up at the late afternoon sun and thinking, *I'm free, I'm free.* Then suddenly I felt very lost. It was as though I had been on a very tight string and now that the string was cut I might be picked up and tossed away.

That was a bad time for me all around because a few weeks before I left *World* and *Fantasticks* New York was hit with a flu epidemic. I caught it, but it lingered on because I worked on. Plus I was still working with Henry on the nightclub act after the show every evening and I got "walking pneumonia" which I didn't know I had until a day or so after *Woolf* closed. I finally took myself to my doctor and she said, "You have a choice. Either you go to the hospital or take two weeks in the Virgin Islands." Naturally, I chose the Virgin Islands. I got clutched at the idea of spending money, but hospitals aren't cheap, either.

Living on grits was not something I wanted ever to know again, and letting go of money was like pulling out fingernails. Being so economical I took the night flight, naturally. I was terrified the plane would crash so I thought if it did, I wouldn't have to pay for all the clothes I bought for the trip and if it didn't I'd be so happy I wouldn't begrudge myself for buying them.

Being nervous about the trip I wanted to get to the airport early so friends drove me out. We had a drink to toast a pleasant trip, a quick recovery and they left. It was eight o'clock when we arrived, but my plane wasn't due to leave until eleven so I had dinner, a beer (I wasn't fancy enough to order wine) with my steak, an after-dinner drink with my coffee and then walked around the airport until ten thirty, at which time I promptly took a Dramamine so I wouldn't get airsick and then, zonk, everything hit me. I was afraid to lie down for fear I'd go to sleep and miss the plane. Our flight was delayed until three and I was still standing.

A lady dressed all in white came up to me. "Do you speak English?" Well, I hardly looked Latin, but I nodded. She was in some outfit. White pants, white jacket and a white fur. A very mousey-looking girl stood beside her and she drew the girl nearer to us. "We're flying on your plane and I thought we could sit together and chat to pass the time." Well, all I wanted to do was sleep. By now, after all those hours of standing I was ready to drop, but I didn't want to hurt her feelings. It was a three-seater plane so there I was, in the middle. This lady in white was so overly friendly I began to think she might be a pickpocket. The poor pitiful girl curled up in her seat and did what I wanted to do—she went to sleep. I was afraid if I went to sleep that woman would steal all my money and traveler's checks.

The lady in white told me the story of her life. She was a "high class call girl" and ran an abortion ring in Puerto Rico. She told me she wore only white and drove a white Lincoln Continental. She was taking that poor girl to Puerto Rico for an abortion. Madam Purity gave me her card, purring that if I ever needed a "job" she would have it taken care of. I was terrified of that card because if that plane crashed and the card was found on me, what would people think? A minister's daughter! I was afraid not to take the card because I didn't want to make her mad so as soon as I went to the john, I tore it up in tiny pieces and flushed it.

I slept most of my two weeks in St. Thomas, but I met a lovely couple in the dining room and just before I was to return, I decided to go to town to shop around. The husband saw me in the lobby and asked where I was going. I told him. He said, "If you go to a perfume shop would you buy a bottle of Joy for me? It's a gift for my secretary, but please don't tell my wife." I felt like a conspirator, but I said I would and he gave me the money. Just as I was getting in a cab his wife saw me and asked if I was going into town. Yes. Could she share the cab? Yes. As it turned out, she went with me. I bought a few bottles of perfume for myself and the Joy, nervous as a cat, believing she could read my mind and then I saw her over in the men's section buying bottles and bottles of men's cologne. She giggled and said, "Promise you won't tell my husband." Well, I guess they had an "understanding." That poor man deserved to have one friend since she obviously had a few.

World hired a new Lisa as soon as I left. They picked a girl whose voice was very like mine and who, from the back, looked just like me. For two weeks they had her on, but the audience never saw her face so for two weeks they thought it was me. She was supposed to be suffering from shock and could not bear to look at anyone. In the show she had been kidnapped by two men and raped repeatedly from California to Texas and consequently lost her mind. Of course this story was told by Lisa. On daytime TV you wouldn't see such scenes. After about two weeks of keeping her face from the audience, finally the lady she was playing the scene with one day said something like, "Lisa, take down your hands and look at me." There was a dramatic pause and then she slowly took her hands down and at that instant all of the action on the screen froze and the voice of Dan McCullough, who is our announcer said, "The part of Lisa Hughes is now being played by"—and he gave the name. She played the part very well, but apparently people wanted the original Lisa because the letters poured in asking for my return and the newspapers picked up on it and printed stupid nonsense such as "Where is the real Lisa? She must be an alcoholic after playing Honey for so long." I guess no matter what kind of publicity you get, it can be beneficial to your career. At least you know people are aware of your existence.

After a restful time in St. Thomas I returned to New York feeling much improved and ready to start pounding the pavements again looking for a show. My second day home I received a call from Ruth Bailey, producer of the Cherry County Playhouse in Michigan, asking if I would come out to do a stock production *Grand Prize*. I was amazed at my quick good fortune, not realizing then that it was because she thought I was still on *World* and felt that having Lisa would be good publicity. I thought I had been hired for myself, but on the plane going out, I saw a brochure on Michigan and as I leafed through it I saw my name. "Where is Lisa? Lisa is at the Cherry County Playhouse." Now I became afraid that she would fire me as soon as she learned I was not with the show. That was foolish of me, but that's what I thought at the time.

In those days, Ruth Bailey's theater was still a tent. I performed in 110 degrees wearing wool clothes and a turtleneck sweater. Why I didn't get pneumonia all over again, I'll never know, but I did sweat a lot.

My first night in was horrendous. I was staying in a cheap hotel (still saving money). My room was not to be believed. It had a linoleum floor that tilted, a bed that collapsed in the middle and a window with no shade. My window faced Main Street and there was a big neon sign outside it saying HOTEL, HOTEL, HOTEL, all night long. The light was a bare bulb in the ceiling with a dirty string. The room was clean but it smelled like pine-oil disinfectant. I slept with my robe on the bed so I could get into it under the covers the next morning without anyone seeing me in my gown.

The next weary morning I changed my room. For five dollars more a week I had a nice place to sleep. Stingy me.

Ruth Bailey was a friend of Irna Phillips' and while I was in her office one evening, she called Irna and somehow I got on the phone. We chatted for a moment and then she said, "Should there be a nighttime show, it might be yours." She told me of a story idea she had for me on *World* which sounded great. I knew my fans had not accepted the new Lisa, so I decided to go back, especially hearing there might be a nighttime show coming up. And I knew that no one could ever write for me as well as Irna can. That's one of the reasons she's such a good writer. She allows the actor to build a character and then she writes around the personality the actor has created.

CBS decided that since Peyton Place was doing so well, they would have a nighttime series, too. They realized in my absence how important Lisa had become to the viewers—the real Lisa— so Irna hinted that if such a nighttime show was done, it would be my show. It was a brilliant plan originally. Lisa was to begin a new life for herself in Chicago and bring in, from time to time, the World characters. Lisa would also make appearances once in a while on World. It had been their hope to get their daytime viewers to watch the nighttime series, too, and it might have worked.

Two months after I returned to World the nighttime show was offered to me. The original title of the show was The Woman Lisa, but it was changed to Our Private World. It was the first nighttime soap for CBS and was to be a very expensive production. The sets were exquisite and all color-coordinated. Even though they hadn't gone to color yet, I guess they thought they would be ready.

I got a tremendous amount of publicity but when I read in the papers that one columnist called me a "frumpy little thing" I made up my mind then and there to start looking more glamorous—but I didn't know how. I wasn't buying in the right shops and I kept seeing myself coming and going. I hadn't had the time to work on myself and then Rosemary Prinz, who played Penny on World, suggested a cosmetician who she thought was very good. For a two-hour consultation and forty bucks I would be taught how to wear make-up properly. That seemed like a lot of money but then I realized it cost a lot more to experiment so I went. It was worth it a thousand times over. After that, I knew how to look good every day from the chin up. I still hadn't found my style in clothes, but I was trying. It's like anything else, you've got to work at it. You've got to want it. Well, I was a nighttime star now, wasn't I? I had to look glamorous and chic.

My star turned out to be the tiniest one in the heavenly production. I was hardly on.

Lisa did her last scene on World on May 3, 1965. She was on a train going to Chicago and as the train pulled out of the station the announcer said, "Follow the adventures of Lisa

Hughes beginning tonight on *Our Private World.*" That night, it opened with me sitting in the club car on the train and I pulled off my wedding ring and dumped it in the ashtray because Bob and I were getting a divorce. I had one line.

In the beginning, both story lines were interwoven. My son, Tom, remained on *World* and he would talk of me and how he missed me and I, on my show, would talk of Tom. But they brought in other characters and in establishing who they were and how they would fit into Lisa's new life, they left Lisa out too often. Gradually, the show lost its audience and by the time they realized their mistake in not having me on more, it was too late.

The show closed in September. I was not sorry. Irna Phillips left the show right after it opened and as far as I'm concerned that's why the serial did not work. If the lead character isn't there how can the production last?

The only nice thing that happened to me during that time was a visit from my brothers. What a shock to find them grownup. Jimmy came first. The once curly-headed kid now stood two heads taller than I—sporting a beard.

I had moved into a beautiful apartment on the twenty-ninth floor overlooking this city I love. Jimmy's first day with me was doubly surprising because when I came home I found him on the terrace cooking dinner for us. He made a Southern dinner of steaks, biscuits which he made from scratch, corn on the cob, and dessert. He's as good a cook as my daddy, but I thought that was so dear of him to do that.

When little Charles came, a couple of weeks later, I had to drop "little." Another giant. Charles is the youngest, but he is even taller than Jimmy. His first night with me, he took me out to dinner. He said, as we sat in a restaurant, "Sis, if you want a cocktail you go right ahead. I'm under age, but I do understand."

My baby brother had grown up.

When *Private World* closed I made it clear I had no desire to return to *World.* The only reason I had gone back as the daytime Lisa was the possibility of the nighttime series, but they asked if I would stay ten more weeks and give them a chance to wrap up Lisa neatly. A character as strong as Lisa couldn't just vanish without explanation. So the plan was to have Lisa fall in love with the man of her dreams, a rich man named John Eldridge who lived in Chicago, marry him and settle cozily down to a luxurious life. The end. And it was to be the last of Lisa. I agreed to do it because I felt it only right. I had a couple of weeks free before they began this story line so I used that time by working on my nightclub act. I was ready now to get a professional to put my act together. A publicity agent suggested the well-known Sidney Shaw. He had worked for a lot of famous singers and he was expensive, but I had begun to realize you always get what you pay for.

My new manager, Dori Davis, who is also my vocal coach, taught me that. Before going into management Dori was a singer in many Broadway shows and when I signed with her, the first thing she told me was, "If you want to be a star, dress like one."

I started buying clothes that were priced so high I would all but faint as I paid the bills, but the clothes changed my feelings about myself. It was hard for me to learn to reward myself, to enjoy beauty for myself. I've since discovered that the more beautiful things you have around you, the more beautiful you become inside—as a person, as a creative being. Today I can write checks and smile a lot because my expenditure is a lasting dividend.

Anyway, Sidney agreed to work with me and we got a combo together of harp (Henry Fanelli), piano, bass and drums. We worked at a rehearsal studio all day, every day, and finally Sid decided I was ready to audition for nightclub agents. Then the criticisms began. Every day I was told something different. One agent said, "You can't use your hands in a nightclub act. Keep 'em still." So I kept them still. Another said, "You gotta use your hands. Don't just stand there." So I worked with my hands again. Another said, "Only use one hand. Never use both." Finally I lost my cool and said, "Too bad about a kid named Judy Garland. She used her hands all over the place and never got anywhere." Another idiot said, "You gotta talk more. You just can't sing one song after another." So I talked more. Another said, "You gotta shut up. People don't come to hear a singer talk. They come to hear you sing." I finally auditioned with cotton in my ears and did my own thing.

One day a representative for a very big theatrical agency (I'll call him Mr. Smith) came up to hear me. From the look on his face, I knew he liked me so when I finished singing I took the cotton out of my ears to listen to the compliments. He liked me and said he was sending a casting director from a well-known TV variety show to hear me the next day. I was thrilled. To appear on such a show would certainly bring me other bookings.

Just before the casting director was due to arrive, Mr. Smith came in and saw me in one of my usual satin slack outfits which I always auditioned in and said I looked too pretty. He suggested I wear something much more casual. I got out of my red satin number and put on my gray suit which I had worn to rehearsal.

The casting director arrived. She was young and quite pretty. I was beginning to understand why the agent didn't want me to look too good. I sang for her, I talked, I got more and more nervous so I took off my jacket and finally I said, "I'm supposed to be plain-looking for you. Will I do?" I was half mad, half scared and half out of my mind because I wanted to be on this well-known TV show so badly. She seemed to love my act. She laughed, she cried, she applauded with great enthusiasm when I finished and I just knew I was set for stardom. The next day she called the agency and said, "I wouldn't put her on my show. She's too theatrical—too dramatic."

Things like this happened over and over. I reached the point where I could gauge the reactions by looking at the people beforehand. I discovered if they were not afraid to feel, then they liked me, but if they were afraid of their emotions, then they were afraid to take a chance on me. But if you're just a machine that stands there and opens and closes its mouth and moves according to a choreographer, well you're a robot, you're conditioned to doing a song the same way again and again. So, you are guaranteed to last at least ninety days—

This was a very depressing time for me because I would not trade my soul for an IBM computer. I knew what they wanted but I was not going to be what they wanted me to be. I had just made a big breakthrough in finding myself for the first time in my life and I had no intention of conforming to anybody's idea of what I should or should not be.

It was now time for me to return to World to begin the end of Lisa. I had been so involved with my nightclub act I hadn't given any thought to World, but the afternoon I sat in the rehearsal room with the cast, going over the script, it was like attending a funeral. I suddenly understood what was happening to the Lisa I had worked so hard to get and keep. And it was my fault. I was the reason she was being written out forever. They learned when they tried to replace me with another Lisa that it didn't work. The viewers would not accept anyone else. In a way, it was like committing murder. I gave her life and now I was acting out a plot that would take her off the air into a permanent retreat where she would remain, unseen by her World fans.

As painful as it was playing out Lisa's swan song over the next ten weeks, I believed at that time it was the right thing for me.

I continued to rehearse my nightclub act, when time away from the show permitted. On my last day, I left the studio as quickly as I could because I didn't want to think about it being the last time I would ever be a part of World. We must always give up something for something else. I was giving up Lisa because I could not, at that time, have both careers. The cast seemed to sense my efforts at containing my emotions and respecting my feelings said little other than to wish me luck and ask that I keep in touch with them.

One afternoon Sidney Shaw and I were having a drink in a restaurant after a few hours of rehearsal when in raced Mr. Smith, the agent. He was quite excited. "Quick! Get yourself ready. You're booked in the Latin Quarter tonight." I swallowed my cherry whole. "But it's three thirty now. What time is the rehearsal?" "Six thirty. You can make it, come on." "But I can't sing without the boys. I've got to call my manager first." I ran to a phone booth and called Dori Davis. I told her everything and she said, "No, I don't think you should do it like this. Why this last minute rush? I don't like it." I stuck my head out of the phone booth and asked Mr. Smith, "Why the sudden rush? Dori doesn't think I should do it on the spur of the moment." He said, "Either you sing tonight or I'll never work for you again." I relayed the message to Dori. Now I was frantic and crying. "Don't worry about it. If this means that much to you, we'll be ready." "But what about the boys? How can we get them together this quickly?" "I'll find them. Now get home and decide what you want to wear, get your music together and I'll be there with the boys at the club at six thirty."

I flew home, washed and set my hair and threw up. Called Rose Everett, my couturiere, and told her I needed the new aqua satin outfit right away. It was magnificent and nothing else would do. I had to have that costume. The pants had wide flarey bells and a frantically exciting jeweled top with a matching long cape with mandarin collar. I had to have it. I grabbed a cab and raced over to Rose Everett's. It was still pinned, but Rose got to work, elbows flying, and sewed me into it.

I made it to rehearsal just at six thirty. The boys had been busy charting my music and the ink hadn't dried so they were fanning each piece as they walked in. The horn player in the band said, eying the wet music, "Hasn't this music been used before?" Bernie Hoffer, my pianist and arranger said, "No, she's never sung it before with an orchestra." The horn player looked me over like I had just won first prize in the local amateur hour contest. We rehearsed in a tiny room and with a fourteen-piece orchestra I felt like the Walls of Jericho were falling down every time a horn blew. I did my act and got into my aqua number. They took me backstage and I was so scared I was paralyzed. The stage manager gave me a shove. "You're on."

My act was too sophisticated. It was designed for the Persian Room, not the Latin Quarter. The people seemed to like me, but the act was too long. When I finished, I melted off, totally exhausted from fear—well, after all, it wasn't exactly something I had planned for days and days. Mr. Smith came back and gave me a lot of no-nonsense nonsense. He said I shouldn't have worn pants. A gown would have been better. I flew home before the second show and ironed a gown. Idiot me. While I ironed, Dori Davis smoothed out my act, made cuts and put in more familiar songs.

For the second act, I brought the house down. And my gown I am sure had nothing to do with it. Men at ringside tables were climbing up the stage to get to me. I got a swaying ovation (a lot of drunks around), but the wise Mr. Smith didn't stay for that show so my three-day booking turned out to be a one-night stand.

Mr. Smith decided I should work out my act in the hinterlands. He got me a booking in a lovely little hotel on the Connecticut Sound. I took my boys, harp and all, by station wagon. We were greeted by the owner when we pulled in. I guess he came out to see the kind of car, thinking that would clue him in on what kind of act I had. Well, the wagon was a rental. Brand-new.

I knew I was on probation and I knew the agency was waiting for a report from the hotel owner. It's a horrible feeling to know someone is going to judge you good or bad—and as it turned out, I was the butt of his comedy act. He emceed the show himself and he introduced me that first night like this: "Eileen Fulton is making her first appearance before an audience as a singer. Now let's all clap and give her confidence." They clapped and as I came out he said, "The villainous Lisa on television, Miss Irene, uhhh, Eileen Fulton."

I started to sing but his musicians couldn't read my music and that really threw me and I almost threw up, but I pretended they were behind me and just kept singing. Thank God for my boys. They played very loud.

After the show, they gave me the customary party. They served a huge cake that read, "We Love You, Eileen." They didn't even know me, how could they love me? The whole affair was a farce but I decided to go along with the comedy. So I acted thrilled and ate a lot of cake because I hadn't eaten a thing all day due to my nerves.

10

My next rise to fame came about a month later. I was asked to sing for free for a religious charity. The agency Mr. Smith worked for set it up but he pretended he didn't even know me the night of my performance.

It was at the Hilton Hotel and the place was packed with celebrities and famous actors and actresses. I didn't go on until 2:00 A.M. By then, everybody was showing their drinks, or almost everybody. The orchestra was on stage and when I was introduced —"And now we bring you a special attraction, Miss Eileen Fulton, well-known actress in daytime TV"—the orchestra put down their instruments and walked off. My four boys went out and waited for me. A big spotlight hit the left side of the stage, but I was on the right. Finally the spot trickled around until it found me.

I came out in my aqua pant suit knowing Mr. Smith was out there and not giving a hang whether he thought I should wear pants or not. I had to step over all the instruments the musicians had left trying to look real pro as though I went through a pile of instruments every night as an opener. I tripped

and my Latin Quarter pants got caught on a folded metal chair
and the chair fell across the drums making a loud boom, but I
kept smiling. It wasn't exactly a Loretta Young entrance. Bernie,
my conductor, rushed over and pushed chairs aside and took my
hand to help me across the stage.

Mr. Smith, hating my pants, was still thoughtful enough to
come running up with a glass of water, which looked like a mar-
tini and I wished it had been at that moment. My hand shook a
lot as I placed it on the piano. Then a man came out and
adjusted the microphone, but he made it too high so when I
finally got to the mike I pushed it down to my height but when
I started to sing and let go, it sprang up and nearly cracked me
in the chin. So, I held it down in order to sing, but when I
would forget and reach out with my hands to express myself,
the mike would shoot up again. I finally left it up and they
couldn't hear me so I had to stop and ask the man who had
announced me to please come and fix the thing. While he was
straightening out the mike I went over to the piano and the
spot followed me while I drank the water. That was the only
thing I managed to do without mishap.

The drunks were getting restless. I finally sang out my act and
got a bravo from the back of the house. A real person. After the
act, Mr. Smith didn't call me over to his table to introduce me
to the celebrities sitting with him, nor did he come up to see
me when I sat at my table. Later, he criticized my costume
change for the next act, but I hadn't made a costume change.

I got rid of him in a hurry. Finally.

When I got my first booking with a supper club in Ohio, there
was a plane strike the day I was to fly out so we had to drive.
When we got about halfway there I began to itch on my stomach
and wrists. I thought it was nerves. When we checked into a
hotel, Dori looked me over and diagnosed it as measles. It was.
I was running a fever and really felt awful, but this engagement
meant too much to me. I would not give in to something that
belonged to adolescents.

The first day of rehearsal I wore a turtleneck sweater dress so
they couldn't see my bumps. Every time a musician would ask
me a question I'd gag and run to the john. They probably

thought I was pregnant. Thank God for my manager. Dori explained everything and set the act for them. I kept thinking the measles off my face. To add to my misery, this was my first time without my boys and I was terrified. When they were behind me, nothing could go wrong for long.

I wore a beautiful blue gown with crystal jewels sprinkled about it. The place was packed. Drunk and loud. And adorable. I stood backstage and shivered with fever and fear and felt very patriotic. Red spots, white face and blue gown.

The club had booked a farm-implement sales convention so there were few women in the room. But the men knew Lisa and when I was introduced they whistled and yelled and clapped and stood up, knocking each other down. I felt like a third-grade teacher when I walked out and looked at those naughty boys giggling and jumping up and down and slapping each other, pointing to me. I looked at them and thought what was there to be afraid of? I shushed them. "Now you sit down and behave yourself. You over there, leave that bunny's tail alone." They loved it and they all sat down.

An audience wants to know you know they are there. This one sighed at my love songs, tapped their feet to rock numbers and whistled and yelled on the pauses. There were two drunks ringside, arms around each other and one would swoon over me and fall into the other's lap. They reached for me like children. There they were, ruddy-faced, hard-working men having a time.

Of course the signs of the measles had cleared up near the end of my engagement, but I was still sick. Every night for two weeks I would be so nervous before I went on I thought I would throw up. Each night was like the first. One evening a new bus boy saw how nervous I was and he said reassuringly, patting my shoulder, "Honey, you'll be all right after a few performances." This was my closing night.

From there I went to Galveston, Texas, to sing for ten days at the Balinese Room. We arrived at the tail end of a hurricane. I was told we could not use the harp because the room was built out over the pier. And you can't keep a harp in tune for long on water.

The lead instrument was piano. The conductor was the trum-

pet player. During rehearsal, we got through the first song fine.
I began to relax. I still did not like working without my boys.
We went into the next number and the pianist played only on the
white notes. I thought he was prejudiced because he wouldn't play
the black notes. He played in the key of C—period. Then I was
told he didn't read music—he played by ear. The rehearsal was
a disaster. I sat there hearing and feeling the waves beating
against the floor and I didn't care if the hurricane tore the place
down. I was miserable.

After the so-called rehearsal, Dori and I had dinner at the
hotel and by the time I got to my room I was in excruciating
pain. I guess because I was so nervous my digestion worked
faster than Dori's. We had a touch of ptomaine poisoning, but
she didn't get sick until later. I had the chills, I was sweating
so badly my make-up wouldn't stay on and I felt so weak I
thought I would collapse. I was crying because the mayor was
giving a big reception for me at the club before my show and
I could not pull myself together. I just couldn't stay on my
feet. I took Pepto-Bismol and Dori ordered some brandy from
downstairs. Finally, after about thirty minutes of exercising my
will, I was ready. I told myself I would not faint, I would
not be sick, and I never stopped repeating those words to myself
throughout the reception.

The reception was held in the lounge of the Balinese Room.
I was so late that it was almost over before I had to do my
show. They presented me with beautiful roses and the mayor said,
"May I kiss Lisa?" He did and then he welcomed me to Galveston. His wife was charming and all the people were very gracious.
It was a lovely party, but I could only smile and try to hold
myself together.

By a miracle I stopped shaking as soon as I got out on the
floor to begin my act. Things ran pretty smoothly except the
pianist couldn't play my music. I got deathly ill on my last bow
and Dori managed to get me out of there just in time.

The next morning I had to be up at the crack of dawn to
meet some press people in Houston. I don't know how I did
it, but I guess I have an indomitable will. After the interviews,
I asked the piano player to come to the club and I went over the

music with him. There was one song in particular that we worked on and I showed him where the black notes were, but he had the shakes so bad, he couldn't learn it so that night, I sang that song without any accompaniment. The audience thought that was part of the act and they loved it.

Later that evening, after my first show, I was sitting in my dressing room, downing a slug of Pepto-Bismol, when I received a note that so shocked me I forgot my queasy stomach. It was from a friend of mine whom I hadn't seen since my senior year in high school in Asheville. "Sweetie, do you remember me? I'm Ann Sutton Redmond and my husband and I are pulling for you." Why, when we were children, she used to play dress up with me sometimes. So, when I went on for the second act, I sang a children's song and dedicated it to her. It was a difficult song to finish because when I saw her cry, my eyes overflowed and my voice cracked, but the audience saw what was happening and they applauded loudly.

For the duration of my stay, Adolph, the club's chef, came in early every day to cook dinner for me. He was so dear. He put up a table every evening in the kitchen, made it up and put fresh flowers on it and served me beautiful meals. Later, when I felt up to it, I fished for my dinner off the pier and that wonderful Adolph would cook it for me. Everybody was so kind to me and had I not felt so sick, I would have loved accepting the many invitations to visit them.

My next booking was in Beaumont. I had another problem with this piano player. Opening night and the piano player didn't show up. They didn't tell me at first. They gave me a glass of water and told me to sit down. They gave me the joyous news but insisted I need not despair. Another man was coming in to take his place. "Don't get upset. He plays for the Presbyterian Church." Oh, I had a picture of my music being played with a lot of church chords. Great. My churchy player arrived and he was a nervous wreck.

I had to go on and there was not a minute to rehearse. We struggled through the first song and my next was "Where Am I Going?" and I didn't know where I was going when he started playing church chords on my rock number and he didn't know where he was going either. I cut the act very short and told the club manager I was *not* going to do a second show. He said, "Oh yes, you will." I did. Then, just before I went on, it dawned on me that this poor man was more afraid of goofing than I was so I announced to the audience that Mr. So-and-so who was the regular pianist would not be there and asked them to give this man a big hand for filling in. He loved it and he did a good show. Had they told me earlier that the pianist wasn't coming, I would have been prepared and could have saved the first act that way.

Despite the problems for my opening, the room continued to do a tremendous business. It was a private club and the owner told me when my two weeks were up that he almost hadn't booked me since I was not on *World* anymore. He had been afraid people wouldn't come and since it was a private club, he had to choose the entertainers he brought in carefully. The only other way a person could get into the room was by staying at the hotel. Not only did every member come but literally hundreds of people checked into the hotel just to see me. He said I was the first televison personality to bring him that kind of business. One of the members was a mortician and he said when I was on *World* I ruined his business. "Lisa, you were my worst enemy. I couldn't schedule funerals between twelve thirty and one thirty when you were on that show."

It was at that time the phone calls started coming through by the hundreds and letters by the thousands begging me to go back to *World*. I was very flattered, naturally, but I was not going to do anything unless I wanted to do it. Then CBS started tracking me down. They said they were swamped and bombarded with mail asking for that hateful-lovable Lisa to return.

The letters kept coming and the calls followed me wherever I went. I did miss the show and I did love the character Lisa, but I wanted to think about it for a while. Besides, I had to complete my nightclub tour before I could come to any decision. It was quite evident that people who came to see me were really coming to see Lisa. And the women I met either loved me or hated me. One woman in Chicago, who was seated ringside with her husband and another couple, had behaved through the first act as though she absolutely adored me. She wrote me a note requesting I sing Happy Birthday to her husband. I did, delighted to please her and then, just before I was closing my second act, she jumped up and grabbed my hand to shake it. I *thought*. Some shake it. She had an electric buzzer in her palm and I got a shock all through my arm. I tried not to show mad and I sang "The Party's Over," smiling icicles at her.

On another night, just as I walked on the floor I heard a woman directly in front of me say, "See? There's that awful Lisa now. I told you she was living in Chicago and she said she was married to John Eldridge, who was rich. She obviously left her son just so she could sing in nightclubs. See? That's the kind of horrible woman she is."

When I returned to New York I had made up my mind to go back to World. I had learned a great deal on that tour. I learned how important Lisa was to millions of people. Those who hated her apparently needed to have someone like Lisa to take their hostilities out on and those who loved her no doubt enjoyed her adventures vicariously. I learned, most of all, that I could sing and hold an audience—no matter what the conditions or the problems. If World would give me time off to do theater, movies, variety shows *and* let me return as a glamorous Lisa, then I would go back. That destructive, deceptive, often despised and—worst of all—dowdy Lisa had a new look. I thought it could work in more honestly with the fact that Lisa had gone off to Chicago to marry the rich John Eldridge. Well, if she had been married to money, she would certainly look it.

I did not tell Dori of my decison to go back to the show until we arrived at my apartment with the tons of luggage we had been dragging all over the country. It was a miserable day when we got in, sleeting and cold. Dori made a pot of tea and as we were relaxing after the hectic trip I calmly said, "Call World and tell them if they will agree to giving me more time off and a better contract, I'll come back." Dori was in a state of shock, the show was in a state of shock, and they called Irna Phillips immediately and she began working on Lisa's return.

Everybody on the show was surprised to see the new Eileen

walk in wearing a gorgeous mink coat and a beautifully "mine" hair style. I had come a long way from the tacky little girl who had only two dresses with hanger marks on the shoulders. Being back was like old home week. I had come to realize, during my year away, how much the people I had worked with for so long, meant to me. I had truly missed them. Yes, I was very glad to be back.

As I entered the rehearsal hall, some of the cast jumped up and rushed over and hugged me. Everybody was chattering at once, and they seemed so happy to see me, it was a wonderful feeling. It was like being welcomed back into a family. I don't know if they knew how much I missed them, but I truly did. They are very much a part of my life. When I walk into that studio every day it's like walking into another life with my *other* family.

Cort Steen, who was directing that day, and is a great big man, almost crushed me underfoot when everybody rushed me and he laughed, taking my face between his hands. "I had forgotten how little you are." Helen Wagner looked so beautiful. She was wearing a magnificent lynx hat and a beige lace dress that perfectly matched the color of the hat. And there was Don McLaughlin giving me a warm, friendly smile, wearing a spiffy hound's-tooth hat, pushed back on his head and in one of his usual handsome tweed suits. Santos Ortega offered a handshake, displaying another exquisite pair of solid gold cuff links (he really does own a Rolls Royce). He has fantastic taste in clothes and is quite the dandy. By the way, he is anything but a grandfather in real life. His oldest child is eleven. And off the air there's no trace of the small-townsy, slow-talking Gramps. His speech is as smooth as silk and he is about twenty-three years younger than Grandpa Hughes.

Everybody on our show is much younger than the characters they portray. Don McLaughlin has three children, but they are in their twenties. Don Hastings, for instance, is only thirty-four, but he probably has been acting as many years as Santos (Sandy, as we call him) because he started at the age of six. Don has three children and the oldest is eleven—the same age as Santos's daughter. And Helen Wagner doesn't have children, but if she did, and if she had grandchildren, they wouldn't be much older than John Brean, who plays my son Charles (Chuckie, as I call him). And certainly, in real life we are not like the characters we portray. Helen is a warm, unaffected, uncomplicated person, hardly resembling the matriarch, Nancy Hughes, who demands constant obeisance from her brood. The only thing they have in common is they are both excellent cooks.

I remember one time, just after joining *World*, I overheard Helen giving somebody a recipe for a stew that sounded so good I found myself drooling. I had never heard of peppercorns but, in those days of grits and more grits, I hadn't heard of a lot of things. The first time I ever saw chives in a grocery store I thought it was grass. What did I know back then? I thought how cute of New Yorkers to buy little pots of grass to put a feeling of the country in their apartments. Helen's stew recipe was my first attempt to do any fancy cooking and it opened up a whole new and wonderful world. I started buying cookbooks and began to explore recipes and started my own fresh herbs. I now pride myself on being quite a gourmet cook. I adore cooking for a lot of people and my favorite dinners are sit-down affairs. So many people prepare buffet style when they have a large number of people, but I seldom do. And over the years I've collected some fantastic recipes from my fans. But it was, in fact, because of Helen's interest in food that I really became interested in making the preparation of a meal more than a boring chore.

Knowing the people you work with is the key to giving a good show day after day. You have something to identify with immediately when playing a scene with them. Helen likes to garden so when I first joined the show I knew something about her as a human being, something I could relate to and this way you have a natural response to the character. But there were two people on our show that I found it most difficult to get to know. The first one was Rosemary Prinz, who played Penny. It might have been a personality conflict, I don't know, but it was completely unnecessary. We didn't realize that until it was too late, but all during the years we never bothered to take the time to get to know each other. It didn't seem to matter. Our scenes were always antagonistic. Fine, we didn't have to show affection or concern in our scenes so why should we take the time to get to know each other?

It wasn't until I returned to *World* this last time that we became good friends. That came about because we discovered we had something in common—singing. She has done a lot of nightclub work, too, so it was at that time we began to talk and when we began to realize what a marvelous friendship we could have enjoyed over the years. But, shortly after I came back, Rosemary left. She had been with *World* since the show's beginning—twelve years. There was a farewell party at a beautiful, East Side restaurant and we rented the entire restaurant for the party.

After a lovely dinner, as we were walking to the door, she suddenly ran to me and we threw our arms around each other and cried because we had wasted almost ten years of not knowing each other just because we had not taken the time.

Another person I definitely had a personality conflict with for a while was Roy Schuman, who played Michael Shea, the wicked doctor. From the very first scene I played with him I did not like him. He was charming, very nice, but I just did not like him and, at first, I couldn't bear even to be in the same room with him. Well, I was really trapped because in my first scene with him, after being examined by him in his office I, Lisa, had decided he was going to be my new lover and I had to really work at making it convincing. You can't just say your lines, you've got to find something about a person to love if you're supposed to play a love scene with that person. But I found myself arguing with him, fighting with him when I was not on the set. I was impossible and I did not have the time to figure out, *What's the matter with me? What is it about him I don't like?* Every time he would come into the rehearsal room I'd walk out if I didn't have to talk to him.

One day he came up to me and I thought, *I've got to find something to love about him because I've got to kiss him and throw myself at him and wear all these sexy negligees and seduce him. What am I going to do? I've got to find something . . .* And Roy said, "Eileen, my mother is in town visiting me as you know and I would like to do something very special for her. I've always admired the hats you wear and, well, I thought I would buy her a hat. Could you give me the name of the shop where you buy yours?" Well, I was so flattered that he would ask me and I told him the name of the shop and I thought how very sweet that was of him to want to buy a hat for his mother. So after that when I played a scene with him I looked at him in an entirely different light and I used the idea that he cared about his mother, which gave me something to love about him. Then I began to analyze why I hadn't liked him and suddenly I realized he looked just like that awful boy, Jimmy, back in high school, who threw my books out of his locker and called me a slut. Once I knew what the problem was, we got along fine and became good friends until he got murdered—on the show, that is.

It's a funny thing about my *World* family. I don't see them much outside the studio, but when one thinks of the many hours we spend there every day, we are probably together as much as we are with our families, or in my case, my friends and passing fancies.

I was so thrilled with the way Irna Phillips had built the part of Lisa. Lisa had matured so much, well, I guess *I* had. Lisa is now a much stronger character and I have enjoyed every minute of playing the role.

Lisa's return showed me in my house in Chicago and my son, Tom, a different Tom, packing my bags to bring his mother back to Oakdale. The new me with blonde hair hardly looked like the mousey brown-haired girl they last saw. While I was packing they did a flashback of the scene that had taken place two years earlier in the hospital. I was pleading with Bob to marry me again and our baby was sick. He shoved me away saying he didn't love me anymore. He calmly walked away and I collapsed crying hysterically on the floor and then cracked up and started laughing. It was a very dramatic moment, but it established the stringy-haired girl as being one and the same as the cool, well-groomed chick with blonde hair. About a week after that first scene I got the cutest letter from a fan. "Welcome back, Lisa dear. I am so happy you decided to come back, but darling, don't you see what they did to you back then? You look so pretty now and so healthy. Please

AS THE WORLD TURNS

AIR DATE:	MONDAY, JANUARY 16, 1967	CAST: (6)
SCRIPT NUMBER:	2812	LISA
AIR TIME:	1:30 - 2:00 P.M.	TOM
NETWORK:	CBS - STUDIO 51	ELLEN
	221 W. 26 St.	PENNY
		NANCY
SETS:	LISA'S BEDROOM IN CHICAGO	DON
	LISA'S BEDROOM AT HUGHES HOME	
	HUGHES KITCHEN	

8 o'clock   2 or 2:30

AGENCY: YOUNG & RUBICAM, INC.

WRITERS: IRMA PHILLIPS
                   WARREN SWANSON

REHEARSAL SCHEDULE

PRODUCER:	LYLE B HILL	2:30 - 5:30 Prev. Day Reading in Reh. Rm.
ASSOC. PROD.:	JOE ROTHENBERGER	7:30 - 9:30 Reh. Rm. Blocking
		9:30 - 10:00 NO FAX(On Set)
DIRECTORS:	CORT STEEN	9:30 - 10:00 Tech. Conf.
	PAUL LAMMERS	10:00 - 10:15 FILM FAX
		10:00 - 10:30 Make Up
ASST. PRODUCER:	W. RONALD DOUGLAS	10:25 - 11:10 FAX(On Set, Cam/Bc
		11:10 - 11:30 Break
PROD. ASST.:	DAPHNE PAUL	11:30 - 12:00 FAX
		12:00 - 12:15 Break
COSTUME DESIGNER:	EDYTHE GILFOND	12:15 - 12:30 Notes in Make Up F
		12:30 - 1:00 Dress Rehearsal
SET DESIGNER:	STEPHEN O. SAXE	1:00 - 1:15 Break
		1:15 - 1:30 Notes in Make Up F
ORGANIST:	CHARLES PAUL	1:30 - 2:00 AIR
ANNOUNCER:	DAN McCULLOUGH	

atwt-2812-1

ACT I

LISA'S BEDROOM AT THE ELDRIDGE HOME IN
CHICAGO. THERE ARE OPEN SUITCASES ON
THE BED. LISA IS PUTTING CLOTHES FROM
THE CLOSET IN A BAG. STAY WITH HER FOR
A MOMENT. TOM COMES INTO THE DOORWAY.
SHE LOOKS UP AND SMILES.

                    LISA

All packed, Tom?

                    TOM

Just about. You know, we don't have much
time before the plane leaves.

                    LISA

I changed the flight. We're going a
little later.

                    TOM

How come?

                    LISA

I want to talk to John before we go to
the airport.

BEAT.

                    TOM

How long are you going to stay in
Oakdale, mother?

                    LISA

Oh, not too long, dear.

atwt-2812-2

                    TOM

(AS HE STARTS TO LEAVE) Well, I'll see
John while you finish up.

                    LISA

Tom --

                    TOM

Yes?

                    LISA

I want to ask you something. You didn't
say very much when you came back from
Oakdale.

                    TOM

You didn't ask me anything.

                    LISA

Is there anything you think I should
know, Tom?

A BEAT. HE'S HESITANT.

                    TOM

I had a talk with Dad. I told him it
was his fault we weren't a family. I
told him what you --

LISA IS STARTLED.

                    LISA

You told him that --

                    TOM

Well you did say it was Dad's fault
the two of you didn't get married again,
didn't you? That was the truth, wasn't
it?

atwt-2812-3

> LISA

Yes, it was the truth. But I wish you
hadn't said anything to your father.

> TOM

I didn't know it was a secret.
BEAT.

> LISA

Tom --

> TOM

I have a little more packing to do -
I'll be in my room.

> LISA

Wait ... You Know tom
(AS HE STARTS TO GO) I look at you -
you've changed. In so many ways ~~there~~
~~~~ You'll become
~~meen just physically~~ There's a quietness,
a shyness. I guess that comes with the
beginning of adolescence. You're ~~becoming~~
a young man Now

> TOM

Don't worry about me. I'm okay.
Whenever you're ready --
HE LEAVES. LISA LOOKS AT THE OPEN DOOR.
A BEAT. CLOSE IN ON HER. TAKE HER IN
C.U. AS WE HEAR RECORDED:

> LISA

(RECORDED) ~~Adolescence~~ -- It seems like
only yesterday when the doctor told me
I was the proud mother of a baby boy --

Look what I've he
done to him

don't let them do that to you again." They didn't do anything to me. That was the way Lisa was supposed to look back in those days.

Up until that year I had never had an appetite and would go without eating if I didn't keep a constant watch over my neglectfulness, but when I returned, I was constantly hungry. One day I had a dinner scene to do with my TV mother, Ethel Remy. She was to say, "Lisa, stop picking at your food. Eat, dear." And I'm not supposed to eat because we have had an argument and I am very upset, but that morning during the first rehearsal I took one look at those lamb chops, the mashed potatoes, green beans, tossed salad and rolls and my mouth fell apart. Well, it was a rehearsal so I ate the whole plate. Then, we had the scene to do again at eleven. Again, I couldn't resist so I ate another whole plate. Then, at twelve twenty we had a dress rehearsal and, once again, I inhaled everything on the plate. Everybody in the control room was hysterical. I had had six chops and three full portions of everything else—including two rolls each time. So they asked me if I would please be careful not to eat until after Ethel had asked me to and then I was to take only one bite, otherwise the scene wouldn't make any sense. I promised I wouldn't eat for the air show. I kept my promise but as soon as the scene was over I sat there and Ethel joined me and we quietly ate everything on our plates. Herbie, our prop man, cooks all our TV meals and he is an out-of-this-world chef. That was a Friday show and on Sunday I weighed myself to discover I had gained nine pounds. I guess for all my life I couldn't eat because I wasn't happy with myself. Now I have to watch my neglectfulness in eating too much.

Most actresses don't like to eat and talk with a mouthful of food but I love it. That's real life. Our director adores giving me eating scenes because he enjoys watching me enjoy what I'm eating. But one time we had a fancy dinner scene with Chris, Grandpa, Dick Martin and myself and I was to serve cherries jubilee. We had very few lines in which to eat the dish and then I was to say, "Let's go out in the garden." Well, all morning I tried to get the dessert to catch fire, but it wouldn't so we kept pouring more brandy into it and I had to learn how much to put in each dish so we could say our lines on time. By the time we were to go on the air, we had loaded it with brandy. That was one eating scene I did not enjoy because actually we were eating dishes of hot brandy. We all burned the insides of our mouths because, POW, when I lit it this time we had a bonfire. I served it on the ice cream, but we couldn't put the fire out. I looked across at Chris and he was actually eating the flames which he didn't know because you can't see them when you look straight down, but from where I was sitting I could see the pale blue flames so I ad-libbed a lot in the scene. "Oh, oh, Chris, watch out for the flames." And I could hear the glass dishes starting to crack. Grandpa was the only one who wasn't playing fire-eater because he wasn't supposed to eat his. He didn't like fancy desserts, but his glass was about to explode and the cherries were popping like chestnuts so he started pouring ice cream over them as though fiddling with his dessert, but he was trying to avoid an explosion. "Grandpa," I laughed, "put out your fire!" We were getting giddy on the brandy. We had a cherry smash instead of a jubilee. That's the only time real liquor was ever used for the show, but how can you make a cherries jubilee without real brandy?

During my first year back we had another mishap that occurred on a live show. It was funny to me later, but while it was happening I thought Lisa's demise was about to be for real.

Lisa was supposed to be dying of pneumonia so they had me in an oxygen tent. Well, after the dress rehearsal, they decided to get a new tent because the other one was old and wrinkled and you couldn't see my face through it so they ordered a new one. It was a matter of minutes before we were to go on the air when it arrived. Now, during the dress rehearsal, they had it unzipped in the back so I could breathe, but in their hurry this time they tucked it under the bed tightly, as they were to do, but they forgot to unzip the back so here I was locked in an airtight plastic bag. I had no lines, naturally, since I was near death. I was to just lie there and gasp as the camera started coming in on me. Well, after about fifteen minutes I realized I could not breathe and I began to tingle all over. Suddenly

Herbie, our prop man, saw my problem and he tried to crawl around behind me to unzip it, but the camera was on me so there was nothing he could do, but the instant the show was over, he threw back the tent, slapped me in the face, because I was out of it, pulled me up and shook me. I don't think I've ever been so frightened, but I couldn't stop the show. I had to sit for a long time with my head down. My lips were blue, my hands were blue, my nails were blue—I was a mess. And since our show was in color, everybody who watched that day, wrote in about it commenting on how realistic the dying Lisa looked.

I remember something funny happening during a dress rehearsal which continued over through the live show, but since television hasn't devised an instrument to project odors through television sets, the audience wasn't aware of my dilemma. We had recently moved into our beautiful CBS Broadcast Center on Fifty-seventh Street, but I had been away doing stock when the move took place and they forgot to tell me that the props were now practical, which meant that a stove, for instance, is really plugged in and when you cook something, you are really cooking it. That's why if Helen is cooking now, she is really doing just that. Well, I was really doing *just that* one day to the offense of everybody's nostrils, mostly mine. Now, I always keep my purse somewhere on the set with me and on this particular day, I, not knowing our stove was plugged in, put my beautiful leather handbag into the top oven when the dress rehearsal started. My scene was with Grandpa and I was to turn on the oven, but not open the door, while talking to him, and then make biscuits.

I was chatting away with Grandpa, placing the biscuits on a baking sheet, and I began smelling something very foul. At first I thought Santos (Grandpa) had changed his brand of tobacco. I knew he and Don McLaughlin both used the same brand as my dad, so I thought, ugh he had switched to another kind but by the time we got on air, the smell really had gotten awful. Well, when the show was over and I opened the door to get my purse out, it was lying there, limp and scorched and everything inside was ruined. My lipstick had melted and was all over everything. I laughed later, but I was furious at first because nobody had warned me that the stove was really plugged in.

11

As I no longer considered the show a threat to my other creative desires, I could, for the first time in the years with World relax and enjoy my work. I could now appreciate the show more, respect it more and consequently, *give* it more of myself. Somehow, I had gotten a misconception of daytime television. It hadn't seemed as important as nighttime, but I, of course, had learned on my tour how very important it is and how powerful. Over twenty million people watched the show *every single day*. That's a lot of viewers. Not only was I happy to be back on World—I was proud to be back. And not long after my return, something happened to confirm my belief in my new attitude toward World.

I had just finished tearing my closets apart one evening when Van Cliburn called and said he had just that minute gotten in from Texas and he knew it was terrible to ask me out at the last minute, but since he had never done it before, he hoped I would forgive him and would I please go with him to hear Renata Tebaldi at the Metropolitan? I have worshipped and adored her from afar all of my life. I was already out the door just hearing her name, but reality stuck its foot out and tripped me. I said I couldn't do it because I had a show to do the next day and had to be up at five thirty. I had to learn the script that night and oh, I wanted to go, but no, I couldn't. Van just wouldn't take no for an answer.

"Now, Eileen, I appreciate your work schedule. No one could understand better than I, but this is such a great opera and I must go because she's a dear friend of mine. You told me you adore her. Isn't meeting her worth losing sleep?" That did it. To meet the great Tebaldi would be the most thrilling moment of my life. I looked at the clock. "How much time do I have?" "Thirty minutes." I promised to be ready.

I still had on my make-up from the show so I patched it up, took a five-minute bath, zipped into an evening dress, sprayed cologne all over me, sailed a mink over my shoulders and flew. He was waiting for me in the lobby. I teased him that he had been in the lobby when he called. When we got there the doors were already closed. No one is ever seated in an opera once those doors close, but they recognized Van so they let us in. My peacock feathers were spread full wing as we walked down the aisle because everybody was looking at us. Even the maestro turned to nod at him and a lot of people recognized me too. It was very exciting and knowing that I would be seeing Tebaldi in person had me flying high.

Between each act we would go out and talk with the great impresario Sol Hurok. He would begin marvelous stories that made us laugh and his stories would keep us late for the next act, which was very embarrassing, but the opera was great and *she* was greater than words can express. While the bravos were echoing in my ears, we raced backstage. Before Van had a chance to introduce me she said, holding out her arms to me, "Lisa, Lisa! You bad, bad girl." I nearly fainted from delight right where I stood. My idol. The one opera singer I had loved all of my life knew Lisa. She told me she watched the show every day and had been furious that day because her set went on the blink just as she was about to watch my *soap* opera. Renata Tebaldi was a fan of mine! That meeting gave *World* the final touch to my new feelings about it.

A few months after being back on *World* I went to the Cherry County Playhouse in Michigan to do the play *Any Wednesday*. I now did not look anything like the mousey brown-haired girl who had appeared at the Playhouse a year before with a shopping bag and stayed in a five dollar a week HOTEL, HOTEL, HO- TEL. I was now a well-dressed blonde with a manager, a lovely Pekingese (*my* star, Amelia Earhart), and a dozen pieces of matching luggage, who had reserved a suite at the beautiful Park Place Motor Inn with a glorious view overlooking the lake. The Playhouse had also gone through some radical changes. Where once I had worked in a tent, there now stood an air-conditioned, well-built theater.

The time before, while there to do *Grand Prize*, I had spent all my free time fishing in my faithful jeans, an old shirt and sneakers. People around those parts remembered that I loved to fish, but the way I looked on this trip, they found it hard to believe so they put me to it. The television news people asked if I would let them film me while I was fishing. I said yes. Then it rained so heavily every day I thought they would not expect me to go tramping out in weather like that. But they had an answer. They asked if I would fish just long enough to get some film. Well, that's sort of faking it and I have never liked to do that, but I decided that if I camped it up, the viewers would know it wasn't like a real day out for fishing and then I would not feel as though I were being a phony. So when the camera-men arrived they found me decked out in a gorgeous hostess pant suit with high jeweled heels. They did not say anything but I knew they wondered where the hell my faithful, faded jeans went.

Since the rain was very wet they took me to a fish hatchery. I didn't care about getting wet, but I guess it was rough on those tough men. I felt like a fink taking a poor fish since any-body could catch one there. Well, I caught the grandfather of them all. He was enormous and he almost took me into the water and in those high heels it was all I could do to keep my ground. The size of my catch and the trouble in bringing him in made me forget where I was so I was playing the moment for real.

When the film was shown, they got so many calls from viewers saying that couldn't have been really me, no, not dressed up
like that and insisted it was a put up job. Well? It was, more or
less. The viewers demanded the film be shown over and over
because they were convinced they had dubbed over a picture of
me so what they had thought would be a neat thing to do turned
out to be a very large headache for them. You see? I'm right.
You cannot fool the audience.

I went back last year to do *Star-Spangled Girl* and this time,
I really did some fishing. The right way. The manager of the
Park Place Motor Inn chartered a boat and we had a ball. I
ate my own catch for dinner every night. The publicity pictures
that went out for that one were legit.

Shortly after my week at Cherry County Playhouse in Michigan I began to get singing engagements from time to time out on
Long Island which was great because it didn't interfere with the
show. I am given time away from *World* to do theater, movies,
variety shows, but anything aside from these is only possible if
it does not conflict with the show. So weekend singing engagements are found treasure for me. One weekend the treasure
found was lobster tails and tomatoes—

I was singing at the Palm Shore Club on Long Island one
Saturday night and I had four shows to do. Two for the "Sweet
Sixteen Party" and two for the adults upstairs. I had worked there
before but this time they had a comic who told smutty jokes.
They got rid of him, but not soon enough for me.

My first show was for the teen-agers and I had been asked
in advance to wear a mini skirt and sing rock, but I don't like
minis so I decided once again to do what I wanted and not
what I was told to do. When I went out I said to the kids,
"Listen, my boss told me I should come out in a mini and sing
rock 'n' roll and you would love me, but I think the best thing
I can do is to be myself." I was wearing a beautiful gown with a
stunning matching cape and I whipped it off like Zorro and they
all gasped when they saw the jeweled gown. They loved it and I
sang and talked to them about Dirty Lisa and we had a great
time.

The owner of the club is a lamb, but most people think he's

a tiger because he talks tough. Dori Davis said that night he was standing with her in the back listening to my patter and he said, "The kid is terrific. She's an an-gel. If she wore white I couldn't stand it. I think if I tried to kiss her she'd e-vapo-rate." And I laughed, remembering the first time I met him. Just before the show he came in the dressing room and gruffly said, "What'cha want tuh drink, kid?" "Water." "That's all? No booze, kid?" I must have been the first entertainer who didn't get soused because —getting back to the smutty comic—when I went upstairs to do a show for the adults he was higher than a kite and was in the audience taking food off the plates and throwing it up on the stage. I guess he thought he was being funny but the guests didn't think so and the manager had to replace a lot of dinners.

The stage was jeweled with lobster, tomatoes, salad, and a number of assorted yummies so I got a newpaper and went out and spread the newspaper down over all the mess talking as I laid out the paper. "This reminds me of my little dog. She's not housebroken either and I have to put paper down for her, too." I didn't lose my cool and the audience thought it was a marvelous smack at the comic. But, had I not known how to handle the situation, it could have been very embarrassing. When we realize our own importance, we are equipped to cope with all the tragic, sad, silly events along the way. The trick to making it with living is always to be in command of yourself and to see the humor behind everything. So I stood on that newspaper as though I were walking on the finest velvet and gave a good performance.

This experience was followed by a not so funny phase of being the target for slaps and slugs. I also broke a couple of fingers. I had a four-week engagement to star in *Carnival* at a dinner theater, the Club Bené in New Jersey. I was doing *World* every day and not getting enough sleep, but I was happy and that always seems to give me the added energy I need. I was also dizzy from all the whacks to the head I got every night. My leading man in a fit of anger had to haul off and slap my face, but because he was nervous about hitting me, I never knew where the blow would land and it often struck my ear which frightened me because of my childhood ear infection so I would cover my ear, if I had the chance, with the long wig I wore, hoping to soften the blow. And he would get so tense because he was a big guy and he didn't want to hurt me that it seemed to make him hit harder—not meaning to, of course.

We worked on it, trying to accustom him to one particular spot until I thought my head would fall off and one night he actually lifted me off the floor with the blow. It hurt so I couldn't stop the tears and I have a song that follows, "I Hate Him," and I sang it that night with great feeling because I was in agony and I got more bravos that night than on any other because the audience knew I had been hurt. That poor boy. That was one show I'm sure he was glad to see close. He sent me beautiful flowers the next day in apology.

Right after *Carnival* I booked a flight to Miami Beach for five days and Dori came with me as she wanted to investigate a few possible nightclub engagements.

When we got to the airport I didn't like the way they talked about Amelia's quarters. I didn't want her in the baggage room. I wanted her either with me or with the pilot and when they wouldn't cooperate, I switched airlines at the last minute. Thanks to Amelia, we were saved. The plane we were to fly on was highjacked to Cuba.

I enjoyed five wonderful days of sleep. I knew I had another play to do as soon as I returned so I took advantage of the leisure palm-tree country offers. I was to start rehearsals immediately on the comedy *The Owl and the Pussycat*. I was especially looking forward to this show because the theater, Guy Little's, the Little Theater on the Square, is one of the most fantastic theaters in the country. It's in Sullivan, Illinois, and has a great reputation. Tom Poston was playing opposite me and I was looking forward to doing comedy with him because I think he's a funny guy.

We had only three days to rehearse which was rough because we're the only characters in the play so we're on constantly. Add to that the fact the Hong Kong flu was attacking the city and you had two very uptight people. When we started rehearsing, I behaved like a weird eccentric. I would not eat out because I didn't want to expose myself to flu germs and I would not handle money. That's the only time in my life I never wanted to touch the beautiful stuff but, again, I didn't want to catch any germs.

The day we were to leave for Sullivan I went to Tom's apartment to do a line rehearsal with him and when I got there I was so shocked to see a Christmas tree and his little girl opening presents, saying, "Thank you, Daddy." I didn't even know it was Christmas. When I work I forget everything. Standing there watching them all around the tree was like watching a movie.

Tom and I were to do the show for a week and in that week I was crippled for the duration. We had a scene where we fight over the TV set. He tries to take it away from me and we're pulling it and this monster is heavy. It's one of the old models and very deep so we're having our tug of war when he accidentally steps on my foot. He knew he had hurt me and he got so upset, trying to get his foot off, that he somehow let go of the set and it crashed into my legs, cutting through my dress and slip. I thought I would faint from the pain and I spent my time between the second and third acts sitting with ice on my thighs to keep the swelling down. That handsome, wonderful Guy Little went by car all the way to his home to get me clean ice cubes because I was afraid to use ice from the theater kitchen in case it had a tinge of Hong Kong on it.

For the third act Dori, who is a pro at stage make-up, did a great job of painting my legs which were already turning green and blue, but the lumps showed. By the end of the week I looked like I had four knees.

The night before we closed I was standing in the wings as was Tom, but he didn't know I was near him and I heard him praying. "Oh, dear God, please, please anybody but Eileen. Don't let her know I've got Hong Kong flu." I was so petrified I didn't even feel the pain in my sore thighs. The only person I hadn't stayed away from had it.

The next morning we both had a fever of 104. Guy brought a doctor in and he gave us shots and some pills. He said, "I don't know how you're going to get through the show." Guy had the doctor stand by for us because he was afraid we would collapse, but we were *deliriously* funny. I don't remember any of it. We had two shows to do. Back to back. I remember during the first show there were a lot of people saying, "Take this. Swallow. Open your mouth." And getting my throat sprayed, but that night, for the next show, my shot of adrenalin arrived. Little Eva Norton, the girl who got the role of Sunny in *Sunny of Sunnyside* when I was a child was there and she brought me a beautiful long-stemmed rose. It was like the time Patsy Bruder came to see me in *Fantasticks*. I was told later it was one of the best performances we ever gave, though I truly don't remember much about it.

The next time I did *Owl* was in the spring and my leading man was Ian Sullivan. *Sullivan* like in Illinois? If only I had made an association perhaps I would have been more careful since I nearly broke my legs the last time, but I didn't. This theatre is in Canal Fulton, Ohio. *Fulton* like in me? I didn't think about that either.

Everything went smoothly during the week of rehearsal, until the night before we were to open. In the first act I fall asleep on the couch, having put myself out with the hiccups, when Ian comes into scare me. He does. I scream and hit him over the head with the pillow and then I fall on the floor, but I fell wrong, which is not like me. I had been practicing falling and fainting since I was two years old. My whole weight went on my hand and being a good method actress I used the pain for the scene. I landed on my hand and bent the fingers backward. I didn't want to stop and yell that I was in pain because we needed this dress rehearsal but Ian's voice began to fade away and sparks started flying like lightning bugs and I knew I was going to faint and I thought they would put cold water on my head and it should be put on my hand so I said, "I've got to stop. I've hurt my hand and I think my fingers are broken." They rushed me to the emergency hospital, but it was closed. Small town. So we went back and put ice packs on my hand and finished the rehearsal. All night Dori stayed up changing the packs of witch hazel and ice and kept my hand wrapped.

Dori made a splint for me so that I could do the show without injuring the fingers because I have to sling pots and pans, lift and yank the TV set, throw things around and squeeze lots of oranges. The splint kept my fingers in a comfortable position, but I guess it also helped the breaks to knit because now I can't bend my two middle fingers and the joints are still so large, I can't get any of my beautiful rings on them, so no doubt they were broken.

That same night while I'm wildly squeezing oranges taking out my anger on them, a seed shot out into the audience and hit a lady. I didn't see it, but Dori told me that the lady found it, wiped it off and showed it to the ladies seated near her then tenderly placed it in her purse. Dori said she muttered something like, "This is Lisa's!"

After this I decided I wanted to go home to visit my family. As soon as I could see my way clear to leave *World* for a few days, I left. It was one of the strangest experiences I have ever known.

I had a comfortable compartment and I was sitting there, totally relaxed, looking out the window as the train sped along when suddenly I thought, *What a sad train. What if somebody has died at home?* I couldn't shake the sadness the train seemed to carry nor the fear that was growing with every mile inside of me that something had happened at home. I learned later that at that very time, my mother had called me and then called Dori to say that Daddy's brother Emmett had passed away. I was going to his funeral but I didn't know it yet.

When I got home Mother told me Uncle Emmett had died the day before. My daddy does not believe in a funeral—for himself—and his brothers felt the same way. When Uncle Furman died, they had a memorial service. Emmett wanted the same thing so there was no coffin, no sadness. A choir sang beautifully and lovely thoughts were exchanged on what a joy living is and what a gift it is. Joyful music and songs were sung on how good it is to be alive. The preacher did not break your heart with "Our dearly departed . . ." He thanked God for giving us a chance to have known such a great man as Emmett, and Emmett was that. He was the most fun-loving of men. He was a marvelous cartoonist and always made people laugh. He was the tallest, but the youngest. My daddy is the oldest and the shortest. When Emmett was in his teens my daddy would stand on tiptoe and pat him on the shoulder and say, "This is my baby brother."

As they did not view death as a tragedy, but merely another dimension of being, my family did not mourn Emmett's leaving, but went on about the business of living with sweet thoughts of him.

Each time I go home I am always surprised to see the hundreds of pictures Mother has of me in the living room. No matter where they move, those pictures are put out. I mean she literally has hundreds, all beautifully framed. She doesn't care whether anyone else looks at them or not. She keeps them out because she enjoys looking at them. She has a baby grand piano and the entire back of it holds pictures of me. Not long ago she finally took down my wedding pictures, but every time I send her a new batch of publicity shots, she can't resist, and they are added to the collection.

She said a few years ago when they moved to a new town the welcoming committee piled into her house and when they saw all the pictures they said, "We know about your daughter, Lisa, but how many other daughters do you have?" She didn't catch the dig at first. "Those are all of Little Margaret." "Well, we know you're proud, but . . ." She said it was like, "Aren't you overdoing it?" That got her mad because she keeps the pictures out for herself. She isn't doing it for show. She doesn't use me—she loves me. And it upsets her when people constantly refer to me as Lisa because she said they seem to think it is *her daughter* instead of saying, "Your daughter *who plays* Lisa."

Lisa's shady reputation gets very abrasive sometimes against my daddy's robes. Mother said one time in church a woman came up to her and said, loudly for all to hear, "Your daughter is a disgrace! Did you see what she did to Bob yesterday?" "My daughter is not like that. Lisa is an imaginary character. My daughter is a marvelous actress. That's why you take her role so seriously." Poor Mother. It drives her to the shakes when she is confronted with not-nice remarks about her daughter, Lisa.

Once when Mother went in to Marion to go to the dentist and was in the chair with a mouthful of instruments she looked up to see a line of women circling around the chair, staring into her mouth. They had come to see Lisa's mother. She said when she goes to teachers' meetings (she still teaches) they introduce her as the mother of Lisa Hughes. She said she has given up trying to explain and now just tries to enjoy the moment and make light of any nasty remarks.

Just before returning to New York, I told my parents to start looking for a house they liked because I meant to keep the promise I had made when I was about eight years old. One wintery Sunday afternoon we were taking a ride and I was in the back seat sitting quietly, watching the purples of twilight begin and I said, "When I grow up and become a movie star I'm going to buy a beautiful house for all of us." And Mother turned around, her pretty face aglow with love for me and said, "Thank you, Sweetie." I don't know what provoked me to say that. They might have been talking about the parsonage's needing something or other, but I meant it and so when the opportunity came to buy a good piece of property I did.

Daddy, being a preacher's son, never had a house of his own and then, as a preacher, again, he could never call his parsonage home. Mother is the only one of us who ever knew what it was like. In all the years with Daddy she has never owned furniture, nor has she ever had a choice as to where she wanted to live. I wanted this as much for her and Daddy and my brothers as I did for myself. When Daddy retires, they will finally have a place they can do what they please with and stay put if they want to.

Some months after I returned to New York Daddy called to tell me they had looked at a beautiful piece of land in Black Mountain and the house was a brick ranch style, and they liked it. I knew Black Mountain was a place they had always loved, as did I, so the next weekend I flew out and we looked at the property. I fell in love instantly. The mountains that stretch out before you are so beautiful you find yourself holding your breath. There are seven of them and they're called the Seven Sisters. In the winter they are snowcapped and they look like a princess crown studded in pearl. I loved the view, the grounds, the house, and I bought it.

Last winter I went there and as I was standing on the sun deck, watching the snow blanket the barren trees and hide the rainy remains of yesterday, I suddenly felt Elizabeth Cross's presence somehow. It was here in Black Mountain that her father had crashed, killing them all, but my thoughts went further back in time to the day when we made a snow Venus.

We had been playing in the snow and throwing snowballs as all kids do and she said, "Margaret, let's make a snow person. Not a snowman like all the children do." "All right. What is beautiful to you?" Then we both said, "Venus de Milo." We spit. a lot making her and we were glad we didn't have to make arms because the snow would drip off at the shoulders. When we got to the breasts we were very shy about making those and we laughed a lot. It was growing dark by the time we finished and she was beautiful—our Venus. When her father drove in and saw our snow statue he was delighted at our artistic display. People drove from all over Marion to see our Venus.

I stood there on the sun deck, tears clouding my vision as I forced my thoughts back to the here and now, but I knew that Elizabeth somehow had been there too and smiled at me, happy that I at last would have a home of my very own. "Good-bye, little sister," I said and walked away feeling somehow she had guided us to this beautiful place.

Just knowing I had that house gave me the "security blanket" feeling Mother had wanted for me ever since the day I had the courage to tell her I was going to New York "to be a star." And, in a way, I had done the same for her. Daddy will retire in a couple of years and the house will be there, waiting for them—waiting for me too when I want to retreat and recharge my energy.

The following September I returned to Guy Little's theater, this time to do *Cat on a Hot Tin Roof*. I had made the grade from pussycat to cat and guess what? No accidents. I think that's the first theatrical production I ever did that had a happy beginning, a happy ending and no mishaps in the middle.

One afternoon, while doing the show, a package arrived for me from Mother and she had written on the outside, "Happy Birthday, Sweetie." When Guy saw the package he asked Dori when my birthday was and she told him the following Saturday.

The night before my birthday the people in the company asked if I would meet them after the show at the Red Fox (which is one of the two night spots in Sullivan) to celebrate my birthday. I was delighted, naturally, and by the time I changed clothes and got there it was midnight—now September the thirteenth. They had a combo and as I entered the whole room sang Happy Birthday to me. The room was full of fans so I truly had a wonderful birthday party. Then, Saturday when I went in for our matinee, I found my mailbox jammed with cards and when I opened my dressing room door I found my room full of presents. I was overwhelmed. The party the night before had been more than I could ever have wished for.

That night, at the end of our second show, we were taking our bows when suddenly Guy Little came on the stage with three birthday cakes on a tray. One said *Happy*, the next said *Birthday* and the last *Eileen*. He had three candles on each so that made me nine years old. Great. And the whole cast started singing Happy Birthday to me and the audience joined in.

But that wasn't the end of my birthday affair. Guy had arranged a big party at Jibby's (the other night spot in Sullivan). When I walked in the entire audience was there (about a thousand people) and they all sang, once again, Happy Birthday to me.

Guy Little's thoughtfulness, the affection of the company, the warmth I felt from the audience that night—these are the moments that make your efforts meaningful. But before we can be appreciated and loved, we have got to appreciate and love ourselves. And you can't do that if you bargain with your potential. You've got to be the best in every part of your self. The best that you can be for your self is the least you can do.

Perhaps it took me longer than most to grow up, to find myself. And now that I know who I am, I can love my parents with much more of myself because now I do not sit in judgment of my conduct as the minister's daughter. I now have my own code of ethics, my own moral standards, and if they are not in complete accord with my family's, well, that is my right, my privilege because this is my life. I know I don't have to be anything other than what I choose to be for myself. I cannot lead anyone else's life nor can I lead a life someone else wants me to lead.

I don't feel guilty about not going to church anymore, either. Church is wherever you are. All through college I tried to find a church I liked. Denomination didn't matter. I was looking for something that suited me, but I was hit by the coldness I found so often among the congregations. I tried to get interested in fellowship groups and realized I was comparing the churches, the groups, with Daddy's. I have never found, not even in New York, a minister like Daddy. He doesn't stand up there and lecture you and tell you what to think. He's a teacher and he's not afraid to say what he believes in, but he hands you ideas, he makes you think, to reason and, above all, he's not a hypocrite; he means what he says because he believes in what he says.

I've gone to a lot of churches in my life and many times the congregation tells the minister what they want to hear and won't let him say what he wants to say. I don't think much of that. If he dares to say it anyway, they get rid of him. He's a mere commodity. I'm not saying everybody is like that. There are thousands and thousands of wonderful people who go to a church and get something good out of it and if going makes you feel good, then great and if it makes you try to be a better person, hooray! That's what it's supposed to be there for, but to me, for me, church is wherever I am at the moment. I prefer to stand on a mountain top because it makes me aware of how immense and how perfect the universe is, or by a river because I realize the oneness of all living things, or in a garden because it shows me how beautiful and how precious life is, or on a street corner or just stand inside myself rather than sit in a stuffy church where I listen to people say, "I am not worthy to gather crumbs under thy table, O Lord." I think that's terrible. I think if God does exist, which I believe He does, then you are a part of God. He is The Father. How can you not be worthy to sit at His table? Your own father wouldn't want you to sit under the table and eat off the floor, would he? This is probably the reason I have always called my father Daddy. To my mind, it would rather be like calling him God since his religion refers to God as *Father*.

I shall never forget one time, when Daddy came to visit me in New York, he wanted to see a minister who he thought was a great man. The only thing great about him was his reputation. Oh, yes, he was quite famous, but my dad had more goodness in his little toe than that man had in his whole being. Daddy finally got an appointment to see the famous preacher and I went with him because I wanted to meet the man my daddy held in such esteem.

They had met before, in North Carolina, but Preacher Famous couldn't be honest enough to admit he didn't remember Daddy. He was tall, well-groomed, a big smile on his very sincere looking face, and he used his hands as though he had just gotten a manicure and his nails were still wet. My father introduced himself and Preacher Famous said, "Oh, yes, Brother, uh, uh . . ." "James McLarty." "Brother James, yes, now I remember. Beautiful country you come from. Flat and warm. . . ." I couldn't stand it. I said, "It's not flat. It's in the mountains!" Daddy paled. "Asheville." "Oh, yes, of course. How's the family, Brother James?" He didn't anymore remember my family than I knew his. "They're fine." Then the great man sat back and smiled warmly. "Let me show you my family." His portfolio was quite handy. He flipped out the long chain of pictures. "This is my better half." "You have a lovely family." "Yes, they're the joy in my life. Well"—he got up—"good to see you, brother. Nice meeting you, sister." I thought I would throw up when I touched that pink clean hand. I wanted to tell him off because this man didn't know the compliment my daddy had given him. Had he only been honest and tried to communicate and said the truth. Had he only said he was sorry but he didn't remember meeting Daddy I would have respected him. When we got outside I said, "He's a phony." Daddy got very upset with me, "No, how can you say that? He's a great man." I looked at my daddy's wonderful face that stared at me awe-stricken and I thought, *No, you're the great man.*

I want to be a great person and a great actress and it's up to me and to no one else whether I accomplish my goal. If on my way up that ladder I fall off and choose not to start over again —that's my choice. Nobody is to blame. If I fail, *I* did it. *I* quit.

It had nothing to do with luck. We make our own luck by sticking to what we are after until the dream becomes a reality. And I realized in that year away from *As the World Turns* how important Lisa was to my lifelong dream.

In exploring the character of Lisa I had given myself greater dimension. By allowing Lisa to be a bitch I had allowed myself the privilege of making mistakes and enjoying a five-minute monologue of four-letter words if I felt like it. Lisa was instrumental in helping me to create my own identity. I'm still "Old Girl" down deep inside and very proud to be a minister's daughter, but it was my portrayal of Lisa which launched my career. And that being so, it will be Lisa who will further it.